# Western New York Weather Guide:

## A Century of Sun, Snow and Rain

by

# Tom Jolls

### with Brian Meyer & Joseph Van Meer

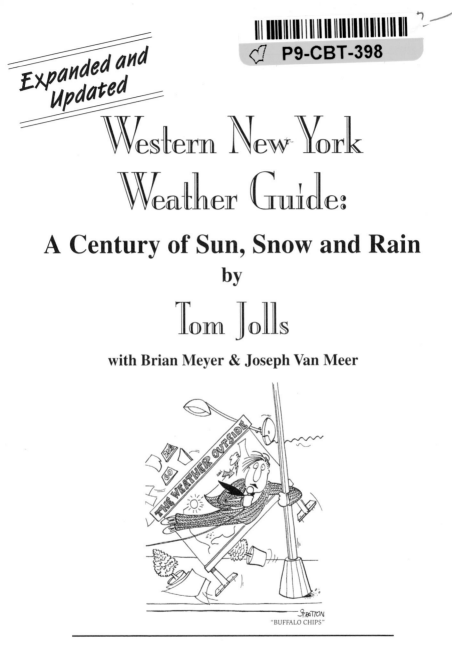

STRATTON
"BUFFALO CHIPS"

Cover Design and Layout by John Hardiman

Selected Photographs by Joe Traver

Other photographs from the Courier-Express Collection,
courtesy of E. H. Butler Library, Buffalo State College
and the Buffalo and Erie County Historical Museum.

Address all inquiries to:
**Brian Meyer, Publisher**
Western New York Wares Inc.
P.O. Box 733
Ellicott Station
Buffalo, NY 14205

This book was published and printed in Buffalo, NY
**ISBN: 1-879201-18-6**

First Printing: November, 1996

Second Printing: October, 1997

# Acknowledgments

As with any book project, there are many individuals who offered invaluable behind-the-scenes assistance.

The collaborators and publisher wish to thank the local staffers at the National Weather Service for their expertise, dedication and enthusiasm.

We also gratefully acknowledge the contributions of John Hardiman, Richard Grajek, artist Tim Warchocki and the entire staff at Petit Printing for helping to make this project a reality.

A special thanks goes to staffers at the Edward H. Butler Library at Buffalo State College. Mary Karen Delmont, of the Archives and Special Collections unit, Margaret M. MacDonald, senior library clerk, and library assistants Gregory S. Galvin and Tameka L. Thomas were instrumental research associates.

Buffalo photographer Joe Traver, who has capably assisted us in other book ventures, supplied some riveting photos and assisted in the production process.

We also wish to thank weather aficionado David C. Lawson for his assistance and enthusiasm.

# Publisher's Ponderings

One of my earliest boyhood weather inquiries had nothing to do with questions about whether an overnight snowfall had closed my school or a steady drizzle had canceled the family picnic at Beaver Island.

"Mom! How come Commander Tom's doing the weather? And how come he's not wearing his uniform?"

Tom Jolls is probably the first person who ever exposed me to the term "lake-effect snow." I started taking weather cirrusly — I mean seriously — as I watched Tom's nightly forecasts (it took me a year or so to get used to used to the idea that Dust Mop was not part of the Weather Outside.)

And so when Tom approached me last year about working on a weather book, I was both flattered and enthused. After some initial brainstorming, we expanded his original concept of a localized weather almanac into a breezy, user-friendly guide which would shed insight on the people of Western New York as much as it would the region's four glorious seasons.

A consummate professional, Tom had already gathered data for about half the book before he even approached my publishing company. In order to achieve the people-oriented approach that we desired, we knew we had a lot more research to do and a very brief time to do it in; our goal was to have the *Western New York Weather Guide* on store shelves in time for the 20th anniversary of the infamous Blizzard of '77.

Realizing the daunting research task that awaited us, I contacted a close friend and asked for help. Life-long Buffalo resident Joseph Van Meer is a self-proclaimed weather junkie with a penchant for digging-up enlightening nuggets of information. His journalistic training coupled with his insatiable appetite for anything having to do with weather made him an ideal research associate. Joe did a stellar job, even as he grappled with a serious family illness. We wish Trudy a speedy recovery.

Without any further "winterruptions," we thank you for joining us on this armchair tour of Western New York's diversity-packed climate.

And let's not knock our weather. As someone once observed "if it didn't change once in a while, nine out ten people couldn't start a conversation."

Brian Meyer, *Publisher*
1996

# Introduction

If there is one thing everyone likes to talk about, it's the weather. I first began to take an interest in the elements when I was 5 or 6 years old. I was raised in the country, just outside of Lockport, in Niagara County.

I went to a two room school house and because there was no bussing, I had to walk to school. The school was about four miles each way. Sometimes I rode with my Dad, but he left so early I found myself waiting outside the school until the teacher arrived. Other times I would find shelter in a nearby farmhouse. The home belonged to an elderly, and rather eccentric gentleman who kept corn stalks in his living room. I didn't stay there often.

But because of the severe winters in the early and mid 40's, my interest naturally turned to the kind of day I faced as I made my way to school. I loved the clear, crisp days as I listened to the snow crunch under my feet. But the blowing, stinging bits of snow was what I really disliked. And no matter how hard I tried to pull the muffler over my face as I walked along the road, the bitterness still crept through the fabric and numbed my face.

And so I kept a diary of sorts, separating the good days with a star, and the unpleasant ones with a dark circle. There were more dark circles than stars.

I recall several times during those days when I was not able to go to school for what seemed like weeks because of the snow bound roads. I recall my Dad skiing to work and later discovering he was skiing over tree tops on his way.

Little did I ever think then, that someday I would make my living talking about the weather on television. (TV wasn't even heard of then.)

And so weather being as talked about as it is, I thought about a book dedicated to weather trivia. Where one could find a fact about Buffalo's weather in a matter of moments.

Tom Jolls

# Contents

# Why the Weather Outside?

Several years before I became associated with Channel 7 the weather was done outside. Why? Because a sponsor who was a local car dealer, thought that's where the elements were, and that's how it should be presented. "The Weather Outside" segment has been presented to viewers for over 35 years. Only when there is a lightning storm do I feel a little apprehensive outside. This occurs only several times a year, and I have an option to come inside.

# The Weirdest Happenings on the Weather Outside

When I first arrived at Channel 7 in 1965 the weather was done live on the sidewalk on Main Street. Number 1 on the reasons to do it there were the passing cars and the unusual setting. What wasn't expected was a car driving by with a guy "mooning" the audience out his window. We quickly moved back to the safety of our parking lot.

Safety? Until we were "streaked" by a young man a few years later. It was a strange situation, delivering the weather and seeing a naked man approaching me. Luckily the camera was off me and inside for local temperatures. At the moment he ran by, he was stopped by security, and forced to sit at a desk until authorities came. He told us how he would have made a $10 bet if he had been seen on the air.

## Alarm

Another time I was in the middle of my cast when I heard the alarm on my Corvette go off. I could do nothing except watch the guard out of the corner of my eye run toward my car. The thief got away, but not with my car.

## Dogs

I love all animals and so when a dog wandered on the set one night, I petted and talked to him just before I went on the air. Then when I was doing the weather the dog fell in love with my leg. Fortunately, the camera only showed me from the waist up.

## Holding Center Gawkers

When News Channel 7 first moved to its present location near S. Elmwood and Church Street in downtown Buffalo, I was taken aback when I walked out onto the set for the first broadcast on the "Patio".

Suddenly I could hear a loud roar of voices as I went on the air. The roar was from inside a building, and it was then I realized the sound was coming from the Erie County Holding Center across the street.

The People were watching and waiting for me to go on, and the greeting came from almost every cell. I guess it was sort of a welcome to the neighborhood.

Even now when I go outside to do the weather, I always look across the street. Very often there are four or five residents standing in their recreation area, looking out the windows. We wave to each other.

# All Wet for the Wedding Day

You might call it the Wedding Day Blues. A Buffalo-area woman called Channel 7 one day to give me a piece of her mind.

As it turned out, it rained for her daughter's wedding day. She held me responsible and warned me that if she ever ran into me in person, she would probably hit me.

I've also had scattered complaints over the years from many local business owners who are upset when I mention storm warnings on my weather reports. They'll say something like: "Why do have to get people all worried? It's not good for business!"

# The Seasons of Western New York

## Spring

Cloudy and cooler than other areas not affected by the cold lake. Vegetation growth is often slowed, thus protected from late frosts. Ice is in the lake, kept there by the Ice Boom. The Ice Boom often delays Spring conditions until late May or early June.

*Courier-Express Collection, courtesy of E. H. Butler Library, Buffalo State College and the Buffalo and Erie County Historical Museum.*

*April 27th, 1982 — A work crew on a barge removes one of the barrels of the ice boom. The removal will permit ice in Lake Erie to flow down the Niagara River. This was the third latest date for the boom's removal since it was first put in place in the mid 1960s. Authorities estimated that there are 400 square miles of ice averaging a foot thick in Lake Erie.*

*Booms Away — Ed Phillips of the Manson Construction Co. guides one of the wooden ice booms into its storage space near Times Beach on Tuesday, May 4, 1977. The boom logs, which were used to hold back Lake Erie ice have been removed and are being stored for the summer.*

## Summer

With little fanfare the season comes in mid-June. Very seldom do we experience temperature of 90° due to lake breezes. We enjoy more sun than other sections of the state. Thanks also to Lake Erie for infrequent thunderstorms, but they are more active North and South of Buffalo.

*Courier-Express Collection, courtesy of E. H. Butler Library, Buffalo State College and the Buffalo and Erie County Historical Museum.*

Courier-Express Collection, courtesy of E. H. Butler Library, Buffalo State College
and the Buffalo and Erie County Historical Museum.

*August 22, 1977 — The fair from the air — Despite the gloomy weather on
Sunday, the crowds still showed up at the annual Erie County Fair & Exposition in Hamburg which is in its 138th year.*

## Autumn

Hazy sunshine and warm temperatures herald the beginning of Autumn. That is why many Western New Yorker's view Autumn as their favorite time of year. There are long periods of little or no rain, it's usually frost free until the middle of October. More clouds are with us in November and continue through the winter.

## Winter

Flurries usually start in mid-November or the first part of December. Long periods of cloudy conditions, along with blasts of arctic air, often bring bands of heavy lake effect snow South of the city. Heavy snow is common throughout the winter, however polar air in Canada and our mid-West are modified significantly when crossing the lakes. That frigid air is warmed 10° – 30°, so rarely do we experience below 0° temperatures. Of course those colder temperatures do happen, but not for long periods of time. I suggest you look at those cold readings out West in the middle of Winter and then compare ours.

P.S. Buffalo's reputation for severe winters is grossly misrepresented, due mainly to remarks made by national TV celebrities who have no idea of what they speak.

*Courier-Express Collection, courtesy of E. H. Butler Library, Buffalo State College and the Buffalo and Erie County Historical Museum.*

*1966 — Spectators gather around the Casino to watch events in Fourth Annual Winter Carnival at Delaware Park. 12,000 attended Winter Carnival opening.*

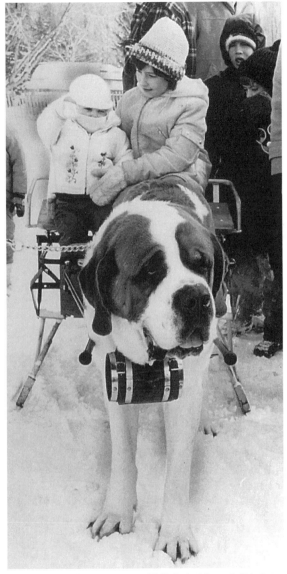

*Courier-Express Collection, courtesy of E. H. Butler Library, Buffalo State College and the Buffalo and Erie County Historical Museum.*

*January 23, 1978 — Chestnut Ridge Carnival — A record 25,000 persons attended the fifth annual Winter Carnival in Chestnut Ridge Park Sunday. Among those who participated were Laura Kohlhas of Springville and Tracy Talbot of Hamburg who were pulled on a sled by "Tim," a big friendly St. Bernard.*

*Courier-Express Collection, courtesy of E. H. Butler Library, Buffalo State College and the Buffalo and Erie County Historical Museum.*

*Peolple enjoying WNY.*

Western New York is situated in a rather unique place. Sandwiched between Lakes Erie and Ontario. The lakes have a definite effect on our everyday weather.

Lakes Erie and Ontario act as giant air conditioners for WNY in the summer. That is the reason Buffalo has never reached 100 degrees. On the other side of the ledger the warm lake waters set up the lake effect snow squalls we have learned to live with. Whenever I give a forecast for lake effect snow south of the city, many southtown merchants will call and plead that I say snow is forecast for the ski areas. Otherwise, they claim, shoppers stay home for fear they will become snowbound or caught in a blizzard.

Lake Erie offers no resistance to the sometimes strong wind as it pushes toward the Queen City, therefore, the windy conditions that often prevail. Because Lake Ontario is so deep, it never freezes over.

In the following pages you will find a smorgasbord of true-to-life tales about Western New Yorkers and their encounters with weather. Read on!

# Blizzard of '77

How vividly I remember the Blizzard Of 77! The storm began on a Friday.

I knew I could get into work because my eldest son had a four wheel drive truck, but I also knew my co-worker Rick Azar would have a tough time with the elements.

I called Rick and suggested he request an Amherst police car to bring him to my place, about twenty miles away. When he arrived my son drove us to the Channel 7 studios on Main Street.

Even though it was early, 2 p.m., the trip was dangerous. It was slippery and difficult to see in the blinding, whirling snow. I later learned that all that blowing snow was not from snow falling from the sky, but was snow piled on frozen Lake Erie. This snow was picked up by the horrendous wind, and deposited on the city.

As I delivered the weather at 11 p.m. that night, I remember an ambulance traveling on Main Street, and I recall the words I said. "Pity the person who needs an ambulance on a night like tonight, but fortunate there was a driver who could traverse the street to take the person to medical help."

After work, what a harrowing trip down Main Street we had! We saw a snowmobile cutting through the deep snow on Main Street. We were grateful we were riding in a four-wheel drive vehicle. But even with that powerful vehicle, it was a trip worth remembering.

My son, Dale, stopped on the way at Eggertsville Hose Company, where he was a volunteer fireman, to see if he and his truck were needed for any emergency in the town. No call was necessary. After depositing Rick at his house in East Amherst, we made our way home. It took nearly an hour to get there.

The next morning the wind continued its unrelentless assault, whipping snow into mountains of trouble. Our next door neighbors had left their home to stay with us. The Guerra's house, the way it was positioned, bore the brunt of the wind and the house wouldn't warm up. We placed a blanket in our entrance so the family room would be shielded by the cold drafts. Our fireplace made the room toasty warm, and that's where we stayed a good portion of the weekend.

About noon on that Saturday, my neighbor Joe and I decided we needed a case of beer. We asked my son Dale (the one with the four-wheel drive vehicle) to drive us to the nearby store. Dale answered firmly with a "no way." He felt his truck might be needed for an emergency. A case of beer was not an emergency. So Joe and I walked to the store and we managed to lug the case back home.

I worried about the load of snow on the roof. So my soon-to-be son-in-law, Jim Bilson, volunteered to go up on the roof to do the job.

I earlier mentioned the family room fireplace. In the excitement of the day, and with the snow depth, I decided I'd burn some papers in the fireplace. In the debris was a milk carton. The carton burned so fiercely, it caught the metal chimney on fire. The pipe turned bright red. My wife Jan and I panicked and called the fire department! Jan realized that the beds weren't made, so she fled upstairs to do the task, fearing she'd be embarrassed if the firemen entered the house. The glow disappeared and we cancelled the call. Needless to say I never put a milk carton in the fireplace again.

The evenings that weekend were made more enjoyable by making pizzas and watching "Roots." By Sunday the wind had not abated. My wife, our three daughters and three sons decided we'd try to get to 11 a.m. mass at St. Leo's. We piled into Dale's truck sitting on laps, we made our way. The streets weren't so bad, so we had no trouble with our short journey. By watching TV, we realized how fortunate we were to all be home and not stranded someplace as thousands were.

On Monday the wind had subsided and I went to work. I had to be at the studio by 3 p.m. to do Commander Tom "live." Things slowly got back to normal.

# Braving the Infamous Blizzard

## Western New Yorkers Show their Mettle

"There was no night, there was no day."

That's how one Western New Yorker described the region's most notorious weather ordeal.

When Buffalo Streets Commissioner James Lindner was informed that his crews couldn't even manage to keep Niagara Square and City Hall free of snow, he reportedly wailed: "We can't lose the square! That's it! That's the city! We never lose the square!"

Perhaps Buffalo Police Commissioner Thomas Blair best summed-up the side effects that the infamous blizzard had on local residents.

"This storm covered the entire spectrum of human response. It brought out the best, and worst, in people," he observed.

Courier-Express Collection, courtesy of E. H. Butler Library, Buffalo State College
and the Buffalo and Erie County Historical Museum.

*Street in front of Buffalo's No. 1 citizen could use plowing as it passes Mayor
Makowski's home . . . Roseville St. has cars parked on both sides, with ruts
in the middle.*

## Slices of Life From the Blizzard . . .

Many Good Samaritans surfaced during the snow emergency. The
late Jim McLaughlin, one of the region's most respected radio news
hounds, was suffering from an abscessed tooth just as the blizzard
sunk it's frigid fangs into the region.

Danny Neaverth, then the morning man at WKBW, mentioned
McLaughlin's agonizing plight on the air. Moments later, a local
dentist phoned-in and offered to trek to the studios with a portable
tooth care kit.

"I had visions of one of these snake-oil dentists coming in and
yanking out my tooth. You know, the Painless Peter Potter-type. I said
'thanks, but no thanks,'" McLaughlin recalled many years later.

He eventually braved the elements and travelled a couple miles
to Buffalo General Hospital. The troublesome tooth was taken care of
by a chap named Dr. Mash.

\* \* \*

If they call Buffalo "the city of Good Neighbors," what should we
christen Grand Island? One National Guardsman related a unique
dilemma that surfaced during clean-up duty.

"The people on Grand Island were so glad to see our men, they were chasing them down the road with thermoses of coffee and food. It got to be a safety hazard. We had to ask them to keep away from the machines."

*   *   *

Stranded cars were also major headaches for the region's plowing brigade. Thousands of vehicles were buried beneath the snow. According to a report prepared by the U.S. Army Corps of Engineers, someone asked one plow operator if he was worried about hitting cars.

"Volkswagens are okay," he responded matter-of-factly. "They go straight through the rotary blades."

*   *   *

The blizzard even shattered old traditions: for the first time in it's history, the downtown Buffalo YMCA opened its rooms and showers to women.

*   *   *

Several days after the blizzard hit, President Jimmy Carter sent his son, Chip, to Buffalo to conduct a fact-finding expedition. Local leaders had been pleading for federal disaster assistance. Some weren't impressed that the president had sent his son.

*Courier-Express Collection, courtesy of E. H. Butler Library, Buffalo State College and the Buffalo and Erie County Historical Museum.*

*February 1, 1977 — Delaware at Utica.*

Courier-Express Collection, courtesy of E. H. Butler Library, Buffalo State College
and the Buffalo and Erie County Historical Museum.

*January 25, 1977.*

"What's Chip Carter going to do here? Shovel snow?" One cynical government official was heard muttering.

But it must have helped; President Carter eventually declared the region a federal disaster area.

\*   \*   \*

The blizzard brought out the worst in some people. Looting became a nagging problem, as thieves took hundreds of thousands of dollars in goods from storefronts and trucks. Looters even lifted medical supplies from ambulances and equipment from stalled fire engines.

One local gun shop owner decided not to take any chances. He posted this warning in his store window:

"Trespassers will be shot, survivors will be prosecuted."

\*   \*   \*

And some opportunists engaged in shameless price-gouging during the blizzard. Some stores were selling half-gallon jugs of milk for $2.50. Eggs were going for $2.50 per dozen in some shops. And some private plow operators were charging $10-per-minute to clear driveways.

\*   \*   \*

Western New York was never the same after the ferocious Blizzard of '77, which took 23 lives and cost nearly $300 million in damage.

Courier-Express Collection, courtesy of E. H. Butler Library, Buffalo State College
and the Buffalo and Erie County Historical Museum.

Kissing Bridge.

And no one is sure if the tab included the cost of search efforts for three intrepid reindeer which managed to escape from the Buffalo Zoo at the height of the storm. They were later recaptured as they roamed the ice-covered streets of North Buffalo!

# Blizzard Trivia

1. How many consecutive nights did the Queen City make the national news with storm-related stories in 1977?

2. The "Red Bessie" played a key role during the Blizzard of '77. What was it?

3. How many cars were towed off Buffalo streets during the seven-day emergency (to the nearest thousand)?

4. Chuck Marino, the man who invented the popular "Blizzard of '77" board game, was employed in what type of work when he hit upon the game concept?

5. How many tons of food did the Red Cross distribute during the infamous blizzard?

6. How did Robert Bahr gain fame?

7. According to the U.S. Army Corps of Engineers, how many local residents were actually stranded during the blizzard?

8. Who was mayor of Buffalo during the blizzard?

9. To the nearest hour, what time did the blizzard hit on Friday, January 28?

10. What was the most popular television fare in the nation during the Blizzard?

**Answers:** 1. 11, 2. The Salvation Army canteen, 3. 7,000, 4. Cab driver, 5. Five ton, 6. He based a book on the Blizzard of '77, 7. Approximately 13,000, 8. Stan Makowski, 9. 11 a.m. (11:10), 10. Roots.

# The Blizzard of January 1982

This one "snuck" up on us. It wasn't as long in duration as the Blizzard in 1977, but it still packed a mean punch to the area. Frigid air, high winds, and more than 14 inches of snow on Sunday January 10, 1982, led Donald E. Wuerch, chief forecaster at the Buffalo National Weather service to issue a "Blizzard Warning" for the area at 10 p.m. Though localized in nature, it didn't always have the sustained wind criteria necessary for a blizzard designation. Sustained winds over 35 mph were recorded in other areas beside the airport weather office. Gusts at times peaked up to 64.1 mph at the Buffalo Coast Guard base. But anyone who was caught in the storm would tell you it was as severe as any other Blizzard that hit the area.

It was a traditional "lake effect" storm that was centered in the Hudson Bay region in Canada. The cold polar wind picked up moisture from the unfrozen Lake Erie, and delivered snow to the immediate Buffalo area.

The Father Baker bridge and Skyway were closed. Police officials had to rescue 18 people from the bridge using rope so they wouldn't blow off the high expanse. Luckily it was a Sunday, and many

*Courier-Express Collection, courtesy of E. H. Butler Library, Buffalo State College and the Buffalo and Erie County Historical Museum.*

*January 11, 1982 — Sub-zero temperatures and wind-driven snow didn't stop jogger John Driscoll of Clarence, who lopes down Wehrle Drive on his daily run.*

Buffalonians were home enjoying the National Fotball League playoff game between the San Francisco 49'ers and Dallas Cowboys waiting anxiously to see which team would go on to play in Super Bowl XVI.

But many hockey fans weren't so lucky. About 300 Sabres diehards were stranded at the Aud after a face-off between Buffalo and the Los Angeles Kings. Some good samaritans opened their homes to the many stranded, much as they did during the Blizzard of 1977.

Hundreds of abandoned cars clogged city streets creating the usual major headaches for the Streets and Sanitation Department's plow drivers.

Many Metro Bus drivers couldn't get out of their own driveways. Hence, public transit was plagued by lengthy delays. The NFTA limited service to city boundaries. At one time there were only 80 buses in service, compared to the normal 300.

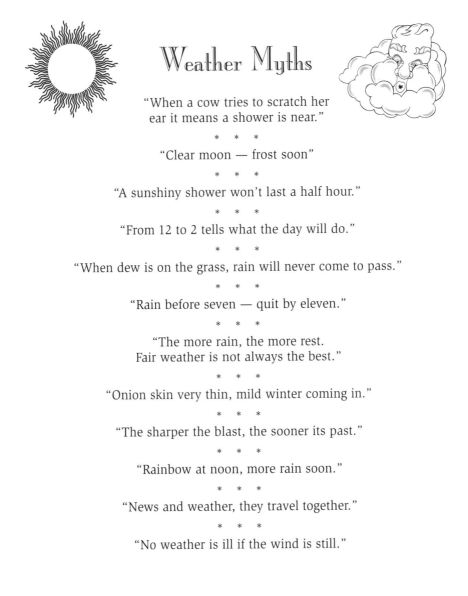

# Weather Myths

"When a cow tries to scratch her ear it means a shower is near."

\*   \*   \*

"Clear moon — frost soon"

\*   \*   \*

"A sunshiny shower won't last a half hour."

\*   \*   \*

"From 12 to 2 tells what the day will do."

\*   \*   \*

"When dew is on the grass, rain will never come to pass."

\*   \*   \*

"Rain before seven — quit by eleven."

\*   \*   \*

"The more rain, the more rest.
Fair weather is not always the best."

\*   \*   \*

"Onion skin very thin, mild winter coming in."

\*   \*   \*

"The sharper the blast, the sooner its past."

\*   \*   \*

"Rainbow at noon, more rain soon."

\*   \*   \*

"News and weather, they travel together."

\*   \*   \*

"No weather is ill if the wind is still."

Deja Vu . . .

# The Blizzard of '85

"Say a prayer for a mild winter."

Buffalo Mayor Jimmy Griffin was a devoted churchgoer, but his prayers didn't seem to work in the winter of 1985. A few months after Hizzoner's religious utterance, Mother Nature walloped the region with a humdinger of a blizzard.

It was during this wintry bout that the city's feisty, ever-quotable leader delivered his most famous line. He offered snow-bound residents a survival tip:

"Stay inside, grab a six-pack and watch a good football game," Griffin said.

As if the wicked weather wasn't enough of a challenge, Buffalo was without a streets commissioner. The mayor and the Common Council were embroiled in a bitter feud. On 12 separate occasions, lawmakers rejected the mayor's executive assistant, Joseph Scinta for the high-profile post.

By default, Griffin became the commander of the city's snow-fighting fleet. He later told some folks that his days at the helm of the plowing brigade were among the most memorable moments of his 16 year stint as mayor.

Griffin received mixed reviews for his blizzard-busting prowess. And he never regretted making his six-pack proclamation.

*Joe Traver*

"I'm proud of the statement," Hizzoner later said. "You get a blizzard here in Buffalo, you have to get off the street . . . I'll probably (give the advice) again."

And he did. Many times during his tenure as mayor.

The Blizzard of '85 took a significant economic toll, causing extensive property damage. In one mishap, the weight of the snow caused the marquee of the historic Allendale Theater to crash to the sidewalk. Fortunately, no one was hurt. And there even turned out to be a silver lining to this snow cloud: the accident revealed a long-forgotten row of antique stained glass windows that once graced the entrance of this fine arts mecca.

How did the Blizzard of '85 stack up against the infamous storm which socked the region eight years earlier? These informational tidbits were gleaned from the Buffalo Weather Station:

|  | 1977 (Jan. 28-31) | 1985 (Jan. 18-21) |
|---|---|---|
| **Amount of previous snowfall** | 33 inches | 7 inches |
| **Snowfall during storm** | 9.6 inches | 33.2 inches |
| **Lowest temperature** | – 7 degrees F. | –10 degrees F. |
| **Highest wind gusts** | 69 mph | 53 mph |
| **Condition of the Lake** | Frozen | Not Frozen |

Many Western New Yorkers who braved both storms said there was no comparison; the '77 blizzard was more devastating by far. Still, Buffalo's Blizzard of 1985 made headlines across the world. A German television station even ran a report which chronicled the region's clean-up efforts.

**In the wake of the ferocious 1985 storm, Brian Meyer penned this column for the *Buffalo Rocket* and the *West Side Times*.**

# An Elevated View

Poets of the past huddled near their heavenly porthole, peering down at Western New York's wintry curse.

*"Announced by all the trumpets of the sky, arrives the snow."*

A faint smile appeared on the face of Ralph Waldo Emerson. A contented gaze; one that hinted he may have been reflecting upon winters past in his native Boston.

Emerson and his literary friends were spying, not on Boston, but on Buffalo. They watched in silent awe as 38 inches of snow blanketed the region, transforming a normally fast-paced society into a dormant white wilderness. They watched as the city's snow-slayers fought the blizzard with all their weapons. They witnessed the coming of the National Guard. And they saw the snow . . . continue to fall.

Conrad Aiken had every right to be spellbound by the snowy scenario below. This writer lived much of his life in his native Georgia where squalls are freak occurrences. Nor were blizzards a reality in his current celestial habitat.

*"The whole world is a vast moving screen of snow — but even now it said peace, it said remoteness, it said cold, it said sleep."*

Schools shut down for a week. The business community hung *"Closed"* signs on all doors. Driving bans were imposed in many cities, towns and villages, including Buffalo. Still, many motorists chose to brave the bone-chilling cold and howling winds that gave birth to deadly whiteouts. Shakespeare stared at this snowy spectacle.

*"Blow, blow thou winter wind."*

Forever an admirer of drama, this was one *Winter's Tale* that Shakespeare had never imagined. He couldn't help but respect both the swirling snow and man's determination to master it.

Nearly 250 vehicles took part in this blizzard battle. The commander: James Griffin who urged citizens not to take the chaos too seriously and to "get out a six-pack."

Mother Nature was no ally in this dig out mission. The snow and frigid temperatures simply refused to retreat.

As the Blizzard of '85 tightened its frosty grip on Western New York, it reshaped the lives of more than a million people. Hundreds flocked to the Salvation Army for emergency food rations. So many showed up that the agency was forced to halt the handouts. Thousands of fuming motorists phoned AAA in hopes of finding help for ailing autos. The airport was shutdown. Metrobusses stopped running. Indeed, life had changed radically. And the leering literary types from above watched it all.

They saw the political storm that the blizzard generated. On the very day that commander Griffin's forces declared victory against Old Man Winter, common council members dubbed the clean up a snow-fighting "scam." They vehemently disputed claims that plows had come to the rescue of every snow-choked side street. They accused the mayor of misleading Buffalonians and blasted him for failing to follow a clear-cut plowing game plan.

Angry lawmakers waived long lists in the faces of plowing coordinators. The lists allegedly documented scores of streets that remained buried by January's dumping deed. One frustrated council member shouted that he could build an igloo on his street.

That proclamation caused Samuel Taylor Coleridge to chuckle. As he watched this snow-dominated soap opera from his heavenly window, he recited a verse that he composed nearly two centuries ago:

*"The ice was here, the ice was there,*
*The ice was all around,*
*It cracked and growled and roared and howled,*
*Like noises in a swound."*

Some suburbs stepped forward to help Buffalo in its unburying project. Others refused to lend equipment to the Queen City, claiming they had too much road work to do in their own localities.

The blizzard gave birth to a massive ice jam at the Niagara River's east channel, causing flooding of unprecedented proportions in sections of Wheatfield, Grand Island and the City of Tonawanda. Some residents blamed the controversial ice boom for the flooding, claiming the snake-like device prevented a free flow of ice down the river.

A plea was made for federal disaster dollars as troops of Buffalo blizzard-busters continued to patiently chisel away at the icy mountains that dotted every street.

But winter won't last forever. The Blizzard of '85 will soon live in history books (and probably on game boards.)

The peeping poets realized that winter's grip would soon weaken. Anna Akhmatova remembered how the season affected life in her Russian hometown. And as she recited a line from the past, it was clear that she also remembered winter's demise.

*"May the melting snow, like teardrops, slowly trickle."*

Soon, Anna. Very soon.

# The Wrath of Gary

The National Weather Service named it "Gary," and his presence was felt in the city and nearby suburbs on Saturday, December 9th, and Sunday December 10th, 1995. The snowstorm shattered snowfall records both in the amount of snowfall in a 24 hr. period — 37.9 inches, and the most snow in one day — 33.7 inches.

Mayor Masiello contacted Governor Pataki, who activated the National Guard. The Guard assisted Buffalo Streets Commissioner Vincent LoVallo, and his highly trained "snow busters" to rid the city of the record breaking snowfall.

Had it been a weekday, it could have been far worse. Luckily, most WNY'ers were at home watching the Buffalo Bills beat the Rams in St. Louis. On Sunday, Dec. 11th, Mayor Masiello declared a "snow emergency," and banned all traffic until that Monday morning at 8 am.

NFTA rail, and bus service grinded to a halt. The airport was closed for 24 hrs. Government offices, and businesses were closed on Monday. Schools were closed for most of the week after the storm hit.

# The Storm of '97

If you ask Jean, the robins have the right idea.

The woman struggled to cross Delaware Avenue near Eagle Street just as the Storm of '97 was starting to dig its icy heels into our frozen soil. She left her government job a few hours early, fearing she might get stuck in a rush hour squall.

Jean valiantly pushed her way through a raging wind, trying to shield her face from the snow.

"If my husband said 'let's move,' I'd knock him down to get to the phone to sell the house. I'd head south, where it would never snow again," she said.

A few blocks away at the Church Street entrance to the Skyway, a motorist navigated his dented car down the icy bridge. He was involved in a seven-car accident which stranded up to 200 vehicles.

"It was horrible. You couldn't see a thing. It was just a big white wall in front of you," said Mark Cummings, a Toronto resident who was traveling to Cleveland.

It was one for the record books — the fourth greatest amount of snow in a 24-hour period since 1890. Most of us can remember the two snowiest days in history. Back in December of 1995, the city was socked with 37.9 inches. And on a wintry day in 1982, 25.3 inches fell. Some readers might even recall a storm which dumped 24.3 inches on the region back in 1945.

But those were only three times in city history when the snow machine was more zealous. The National Weather Service's airport station officially logged 21.6 inches of snow by Saturday afternoon. Mayor Masiello declared a snow emergency and imposed a driving ban for about 11 hours on Saturday.

"The ban gave city crews a golden opportunity to plow the mains and secondaries. I think they did an excellent job," the mayor said as he stood outside the Broadway Barns, the nerve center of the city's snow-fighting operations.

Streets Commissioner Vincent LoVallo also had words of praise for Buffalo's plowing brigade. But he quickly reminded residents that it was going to take some time to get to every snow-clogged side street.

Travel restrictions were also imposed in the Tonawandas, Grand Island, Lancaster, Depew, Fort Erie and many other localities. Law enforcement agencies reported scores of abandoned or stranded vehicles.

The storm closed Greater Buffalo International Airport on Saturday. Even, Walden Galleria, the region's largest shopping mecca, was closed for the day.

## *"I have a feeling we're not in Kansas anymore"*

# Western New York Twisters

Stunned eyewitnesses described it as a scene out of the *Wizard of Oz*. First came the clouds. Then the funnel. Then a column of debris swirling chaotically in a large area. People could see entire evergreen trees dancing in the air. Huge limbs were snapped like match sticks.

But they weren't in Kansas; they were on Union Road near George Urban Boulevard late in the afternoon on July 30, 1987. A twister packing winds of more than 110 mph played a dangerous game of hopscotch across a bustling business district in Cheektowaga.

For at least five frantic minutes, the tornado peeled off roofs, decimated garages and damaged more than 130 homes and businesses. The most severe damage occurred at the Holiday Showcase restaurant on Union Road where the roof was ripped-off. The back portion of the eatery was destroyed. Amazingly, the front section of the dining area was virtually untouched.

While no one was hurt, the damage toll for the entire neighborhood approached $15 million.

This researcher was at the U-Crest volunteer fire hall moments after the tornado touched down. One witness said it was an afternoon that will be etched in his memory as long as he lives.

"I've never seen anything like it before. It was amazing. And the sound. It was like the loudest freight train you've ever heard," the man said, still trembling from his close encounter of the funnel-kind.

Investigators from the National Weather Service classified it as "F-2" tornado, towards the lower end of a five-step scale that ranks storms. Forecasters estimated that the winds in the funnel cloud were probably in the 113-to-157 mph range.

It took months to repair many of the homes and businesses. But some of the affected establishments wasted no time; less than three hours after the tornado touched down, crews at the Putt Putt miniature golf course on Union Road posted a sign which read: "Cleaning Up — Open Tomorrow at 9 a.m."

\*   \*   \*

Experts at the National Weather Service say those who witnessed the 1987 tornado may have experienced a once-in-a-lifetime encounter. Twisters typically strike heavily-populated metropolitan areas in Western New York only four or five times a century. However, tornadoes hit rural areas on the Niagara Frontier every five years or so. Below is a list more than a dozen sightings in the Western New York area:

- A tiny funnel cloud knocked down trees, damaged barns and scattered debris over a rural community northwest of Lockport in August of 1994. There were no injuries.

- The summer of 1994 saw an unusually large number of tornadoes hit the region. A weak tornado touched down in Angola in June of 1994, snapping tree limbs and damaging road signs. No one was hurt and damage was minimal. Two weeks earlier, there were twisters reported in the Cattaraugus County Town of Freedom near Arcade and in the Cattaraugus County Town of Conewango. About two dozen mobile homes in Freedom were damaged but there were no serious injuries.

- May 2, 1983 — A twister touched down in Chautauqua County, killing two people and critically injuring four others. Damage is pegged at $3 million.

- May 17, 1969 — More than 75 homes, businesses and churches were damaged by a twister which hit Sinclairville. A local farmer was hurt when his barn collapsed.

*Courier-Express Collection, courtesy of E. H. Butler Library, Buffalo State College and the Buffalo and Erie County Historical Museum.*

*Sinclairville — May 17, 1969*

*Courier-Express Collection, courtesy of E. H. Butler Library, Buffalo State College*
*and the Buffalo and Erie County Historical Museum.*

*Sinclairville — May 17, 1969*

*Courier-Express Collection, courtesy of E. H. Butler Library, Buffalo State College*
*and the Buffalo and Erie County Historical Museum.*

*Part of the roof of the gas station is shown in back of the home at 156 June Road. In the background is the Kenmore Mercy Hospital where 24 windows were broken.*

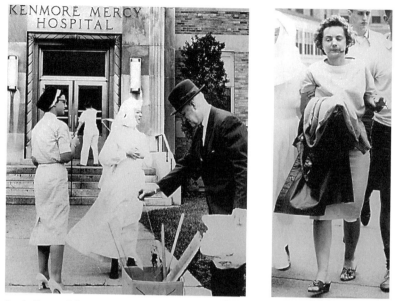

Courier-Express Collection, courtesy of E. H. Butler Library, Buffalo State College and the Buffalo and Erie County Historical Museum.

People near Kenmore Mercy Hospital cope with broken glass and debris following the 1961 twister.

- July 7, 1961 — A small tornado tore through the Elmwood-Sheridan and Sheridan-Parkside neighborhoods of the Town of Tonawanda. Roofs were peeled-off buildings, trees were uprooted and cars were flipped over like Matchbox toys. Fortunately, only one teenaged girl suffered minor injuries. The fierce wind struck her while she was waiting for a bus in front of Kenmore Mercy Hospital.

- April 25, 1957 — Investigators confirmed that a tornado touched down in a rural community near South Newstead. No injuries were reported.

- June 10, 1945 — Six people were injured and damage was set at $5 million after a twister hit Jamestown.

- April 1, 1929 — Funnel clouds touched down in Angola and Orchard Park.

- July 23, 1920 — A twister killed two people and destroyed 200 barns as it ripped through Ebenezer and Gardenville, then continued its destructive path into Allegany County.

   Experts say the city of Buffalo has never been hit by a twister, although tornado-related thunderstorms have caused extensive damage in some city neighborhoods.

# Weather and You

Does a sunny day make you feel better? Of course it does. And cloudy, humid days would prompt some to stay in bed if they could.

\*   \*   \*

Birds are a great forecaster of weather conditions. When you see many birds perched on telephone wires, they aren't gossiping. It's likely the air is so full of moisture, (humid) that it takes great effort to flap their wings. They, therefore, sit until drier air comes along.

\*   \*   \*

Joe Traver

Growing up in the 40's I listened to WBEN's Clint Buehlman who would often sing about weather conditions. I recall some: "Leave for work a little early cause the roads are very slick."

Clint was the only source to find out if your school was closed and the roads that were impassable. "Slippery slip — Sali'de sali'de."

# Western New Yorkers Most Memorable Weather Events

For Helen Hammond of Buffalo's West Side, the Blizzard of '77 was the most memorable weather ordeal. She was working at the Rosa Coplon Home and was stuck there for two days. She explained that she and others had to sleep in an older part of the facility that now has been razed.

"Some of us played cards with the staff and residents of the home, while others read. Finally, a nurse's boyfriend drove us home. My mother was home waiting for me. I felt safe and secure once I walked into my home."

\*   \*   \*

Shari Cook of Amherst, NY also recalls Blizzard of '77. "I was astounded by the amount of snow. You could only see the roofs of the cars." Some friends of hers were stranded at her home so they played cards and enjoyed each other's company.

Our awning blew apart so we secured it with strings so it wouldn't come through the window."

\*   \*   \*

"It looked beautiful, absolutely breathtaking" said Darlene Soemann of Eden, speaking of the ice storm of 1976. "I took lots of pictures. The country settings were magnificently coated in ice." She said that she and her family lost power for several days, and was able to have quality time with her family. They played cards by the fireplace, and had no phone or television.

\*   \*   \*

"It was the Ice Storm of 1976," said Mary Lou Curtin of Orchard Park, NY. She had no electricity for three or four days. "The trees in our front yard started to break. It was frightening" she recalled. "The trees started to break off and my yard was a mess."

\*   \*   \*

For Russell Wansart of Buffalo, "It was the Blizzard of '77. I was stationed in Wiesbaden, Germany in the Army. I was coming home on leave, and we landed in Holland, and I discovered there were no flights to the East Coast at all. The weather situation in Buffalo was constantly aired on German Television."

"I called and got a fourteen day extension."

When he got home Russell helped remove snow around his home and helped his family with chores.

\*   \*   \*

Devon Kennedy, a Buffalo postal carrier remembers the wicked winter of 1995. "It was horrifying, because the streets were all blocked with snow. The Commissioner of Streets promised that the streets would be plowed at least once of snow, but we had a hard time getting the mail delivered last winter. The elderly, and the people who have lived in the neighborhood for years are the ones who seem to shovel. You kind of worry about the elderly when they're outside shoveling, no matter what the weather conditions."

\*   \*   \*

Diane Johnson, Buffalo — "The Blizzard of '77. It lasted a very long time. It was a very bad Blizzard! We had to make lot of changes and adjustments in our household. Luckily everyone was home at the time. My husband Ray, happened to be home at the time from General Motors, he worked the night shift. Food supplies became very low, the storm kept up for days." To pass the time she and her family played board games and puzzles. It was three weeks before she and her husband would go back to work.

\* \* \*

Anne Fraterrigo, Buffalo, Police Officer — "I can remember a long, hot, hot summer when I was very pregnant. It was 1986. It was the month of August, we must have at least two straight weeks of temperatures in the high nineties. I was 7 or 8 months pregnant. It was awful!" For relief, Anne sat in front of a fan and drank ice water. At that time she worked on the fourth floor of police headquarters. "There was no air conditioning, and the computers didn't even like it," she said.

\* \* \*

Russell S. Genco, Mount Morris, New York — Has two outstanding weather memories: 1972, Tropical Storm Agnes, and the Ice Storm that hit our region around 1992. "Agnes affected me by flooding my basement. We were filled with a lot of anxiety not knowing what it would do to the people downstream of the Mt. Morris Dam.

"I was in a place that was relatively safe, but it backed up our sewers, into the basement. I never feared that the dam would overtop. I knew that the U.S. Army Corps Of Engineers designed an excellent dam. I also knew that the Corps Of Engineers would let out the amount of water that would be necessary to stop the back flooding of the dam, and yet keep the level of the Genesee River so that it would not overflow the banks between Mt. Morris and Rochester. They had to control the gates, to maintain the level behind the dam so it wouldn't overtop the spillway, and cause even more flooding."

"In 1992 there was an ice storm that brought down many, many trees. We were without power for a week. This was very memorable to me because my wife, Rose had to depend on an oxygen generator to keep her lungs going. We had oxygen delivered, also we used candles for heat, and light. You would be surprised using three or four candles how much it heats up the bathroom. We did our cooking on a propane grill I purchased. All the gas stations had no electricity to run the pumps, so we had no gas to run our cars."

\* \* \*

Carole Perry, Buffalo — "It has to be the Blizzard of '77. I remember my kids were seven and four, and I was babysitting at the time for two other children. It started snowing more and more, and my son jumped in a snow bank and was completely buried. My husband Richard was working at a grocery store that night in Tonawanda.

"My bedroom window blew in, and snow was coming in so I used cardboard to try to block it. The children's mother never made it back that night, nor my husband. I baked cookies and anything I could think of just to keep the house warm. We passed the time by watching the TV mini-series 'Roots'."

\* \* \*

Nancy Harvey, Buffalo — owner, "Elmwood Blossoms" "There was an Easter the second year that I opened my business. I had all these orders and we ended up having this huge snowstorm. Here I am with all these ordered flowers ready to have a fantastic day in sales, and no one came in to pick up and pay for their flowers. It was devastating. I donated the flowers to hospitals around the area to make someone's day a little better."

Anne Goodman, Sanborn, New York — The Blizzard of '77. She was home with her two very young daughters. Her husband Richard, a trucker, was out of town on deliveries.

"I was stuck in the house for three days, and there was a water main break in Sanborn. We had no water, our pipes were frozen, so I would get snow from the porch and boil it down. My neighbor came over to check on us. When he got ready to leave, the snowdrifts in twenty minutes blocked in all the doors. We ended up removing the storm door, so he could climb his way out of the house. I cooked a lot, and baked to keep the house warm. My husband finally arrived from Pennsylvania on Monday, and I was thrilled he was home."

# The Worst Nightmares of Local Politicos...

## Vincent LoVallo – Buffalo Streets Commissioner

"My worst weather nightmare? That's easy. December 10, 1995. For 15 straight hours, it snowed between three and five inches every hour. It never stopped."

## Dennis Gorski – Erie County Executive

"It was during the Blizzard of '77. My wife was out in one of our cars. She wanted to check on my mom. Her car slid off the road into four or five feet of snow right on the Buffalo-West Seneca border. She called me from a nearby home and I had to walk about one mile. It was bitter cold and I was absolutely frightened. I would have to go back to my Vietnam days to find a more harrowing moment."

## Anthony Masiello – Buffalo Mayor

"It was during the ice storm in 1976. We know how to deal with snow and rain. But we don't get ice storms too often and the storm that hit us in '76 was scary. All the telephone wires were frozen. The trees were frozen. People were slipping and sliding all over the place. It was just an eerie experience."

## James Pitts – Buffalo Common Council President

"When I was a kid, I remember the day when lightning struck St. Michael's Church. I used to shine shoes downtown. You know, around Laub's Old Spain, Shea's and the Paramount Theater. I was on my way home and all of a sudden, it got real dark. That's when lightning struck St. Michael's. I thought I was going to die."

# Niagara Falls Weather Facts

When the forces of Mother Nature are paired up with the majesty of one of the world's natural wonders, the results can be astounding. Prominent Niagara Falls historian Paul Gromosiak, who has written four books on the Mighty Niagara, has researched many of the momentous weather-related events. Among them:

**Summer of 1816** — This season was known in the Niagara region as "the year without a summer" because there were frosts in June, July, August and September. In May of that year, so much ice from Lake Erie accumulated above the falls that the American and Bridal Veil Falls were almost "turned off." In fact, visitors could actually venture onto the islands in the upper rapids merely by walking on the ice.

**March 29, 1848** — An ice dam on Lake Erie, at the source of the Niagara River, almost caused the falls to be dry for about 12 hours. Only a trickle of water went over the Horseshoe Fall until the dam broke. A footnote: The Horseshoe Fall has never frozen entirely because of the sheer volume of water which it receives. However, the American Fall and Bridal Veil Fall have completely frozen many times in the past. The last time this happened was in 1938.

**Winter of 1888-89** — A monstrous ice bridge formed in the Niagara gorge, destroying the Maid of the Mist docks on both sides of the river. In fact, the bridge nearly pushed the Upper Steel Arch Bridge off its abutments.

**January 9, 1889** — A heavy gale caused the Upper Suspension bridge to collapse. Just before it broke apart, its cables and platforms danced up and down. Fortunately, no people were on the bridge when it collapsed. It was replaced by a sturdier structure only two months later.

Speaking of gusts, many visitors wonder why it is usually more windy by the falls. Gromosiak says there is a steady breeze much of the time because a lot of air is forced down with the falling water into the river below. The air is compressed and eventually expands, causing serious updrafts which can behave unpredictably.

**January 27, 1938** — Imagine the stunned amazement of a photographer from Niagara Falls as he stood near the Honeymoon Bridge and watched the massive span collapse. An unusual amount of ice produced by a harsh winter caused pressure on the bridge supports.

While experts were aware of the danger and closed the bridge, most people assumed there would be plenty of warning when the structure collapsed. But they were wrong. At 4:20 p.m. on that frigid January day, only one man ended up getting a photo of the sudden collapse of this historic span.

**March 22, 1953** — At approximately 8:03 p.m., a mysterious object exploded over the upper Niagara River. The explosion was preceded by a blinding flash of light. Some stunned onlookers claim they saw metallic debris floating towards the falls. Experts never found any physical evidence to explain the bizarre occurrence; they surmised that a meteorite had struck the Niagara River.

**Rainbows** — Historian Paul Gromosiak has interviewed more than 40,000 Niagara Falls tourists over the years. He claims one of the most commonly asked questions involves the colorful rainbows which frequently grace the natural wonder. How do they form? For a rainbow to be visible, the sun must be behind the observer and the mist must be in front of the observer. When the sunlight passes through the water droplets, it is broken up into all of the glorious colors which can produce some wonderful "Kodak moments."

# Weather Stick

I learned that long ago viewers didn't care that much about highs and lows and cold fronts. What fascinated them were things like Weather Sticks. I wish I had the franchise to sell these devices. How very popular they are — and they do work!

But how? When the air begins to receive moist conditions the stick absorbs the dampness and falls. This is a sign of rain. When drier air comes in, the wood dries out and rises. Thus drier air, and more pleasant conditions.

The stick supposedly was used by our Native Indians long ago, and are very popular in New England where most are made.

# Tropical Storm Agnes

It was a flooding disaster unparalleled on the Southern Tier. Tropical Storm Agnes, the 100-mile-per-hour hurricane that swept across Florida in June, 1972, brought tragedy and devastation to many communities in Western New York.

Billed as the most extensive flood in the history of the Eastern United States, the storm caused at least two dozen deaths in the region and hundreds of millions of dollars in damage. Homes across Western New York sustained $100 million in damage. President Nixon declared a federal disaster, freeing up $200 million in assistance.

The relentless deluge of rain was a result of rare factors. Agnes came out of a collision course of weather systems that carried a 50-to-1 chance of being so destructive the National Weather Service reported.

Agnes' assault on WNY began as she skulled up the East Coast after whacking the state of Florida. Agnes picked moisture off the Atlantic and hurled it inland, into the cold air of the Eastern mountains. The relatively warmer Atlantic air condensed and the rain began. Agnes unleashed 6-to-10 inches of rain, and was centered over northeast Pennsylvania and part of New York State.

The raging waters of the Genesee River destroyed an entire wing of the Jones Memorial Hospital in Wellsville. Luckily, patients had been moved to another area before the collapse.

In the Wellsville area, right up to the Mount Morris Dam, the flood swollen Genesee River also caused massive destruction to homes, farms, and businesses. Downstream of the dam, "controlled" flooding took place. Nearby residents in Mt. Morris were evacuated because of the large amounts of water being released. At one time 15,000 cubic feet of water was being released per second, more than the flow that occurs over the American side of Niagara Falls!

The release of this amount of water was necessary through the flood control gates to alleviate the massive pressure on the 185 foot high dam. There was even more concern by the Army Corps Of Engineers to prevent overtopping of the spillway. At one point the water levels came to within four feet of the spillway. Had the spillway overtopped, massive damage would have resulted downstream with log jams and additional life threatening damage. Thanks to the dam, the City Of Rochester was spared from significant damage. It is estimated that the dam prevented $210 million in damage to the Rochester region.

In Steuben County, one of the hardest hit regions, the Chemung River wreaked havoc. The Corning Hospital facility's first floor was practically gone. The flooding caused $4 million in damages to a new laboratory and equipment. The flooding caused extensive damage to the world-famous Corning Glass Works Tourist Center and Museum. Losses were heavy when the water reached a level of five feet on the main floor. The Corning Museum suffered damage to rare glass pieces, and manuscripts.

# The Floods of 1963

For Mrs. William D. Richards it was a feeling of "fright, terrible fright," when she first discovered that her South Buffalo basement had become an indoor pool. A series of powerful thunderstorms hit the Buffalo area on July 29, and August 7, 1963.

Buffalo and its suburban communities were inundated by 3.5 inches of rain on July 29, and 3.88 inches of rain between 5 and 10 on the morning of August 7th.

It was the worst storm recorded in the area in 70 years, causing more than $35 million in damage. Storm drains exceeded their capacity, and many cellar walls caved in.

Mrs. Richards recalled that her husband was pumping water out of their Downing Street home. But within a few hours the pump could not remove the deluge of water that inundated her cellar, which caused one wall to buckle in. "We left the house, I remember worrying about our wall to wall carpeting on the first floor. The water rose almost eight feet in the cellar but it didn't damage the rug."

The plight of Mitchell Sallie, of Guliford Street was no different. Sallie's basement was flooded with over six inches of water.

"I called the sewer department, the police, the fire department, and the gas company, the electric company and the telephone company." "No one showed up. I'm bushed, beat and disgusted," the man lamented.

Camera enthusiasts clicked their shutters as they peered over the railing of the Scajaquada Expressway at Elmwood Avenue. They watched as water rose more than six feet. Several cars were submerged in the underpass.

In fact, one of the most severely flooded areas was the neighborhood near Delaware Park. The bridge at Lincoln Parkway near the juncture of Mirror and Delaware Park Lake (now Hoyt Lake) outside the art gallery, had virtually disappeared. It was covered by flood water. In front of the Park Casino the rising water buried the lamp posts, only the glass globes could be seen.

Flooding at the Hertel Rosalia telephone center knocked out service to over 36,000 phones in North Buffalo, Kenmore, and the Town of Tonawanda. Bus service was halted for the first time since the St. Patrick's Day snowstorm that hit the area in 1936.

Still Buffalo lived up to its reputation as "The City Of Good Neighbors." Fire Commissioner Robert J. Zahm Jr. called for 180 volunteers to cope with the flooding emergency. He ended up with 200 off-duty firemen who helped supplement the city's relief efforts in pumping out residents homes.

When the rain cleared out of the area, the sun came out briefly that afternoon. This prompted many youngsters to swim in the flooded streets. Many calls started coming into the police department about the "street swimmers," a welcome departure from the scores of emergency calls which had been pouring into the switchboards. One popular "swimming hole" was at the corner of Parkside and Linden.

Buffalo Mayor, Chester Kowal toured the flooded area with local officials to assess the damage. In a telegram to Governor Nelson Rockefeller, the mayor estimated the damage at $35 million. Kowal said that there was $7 million in damage to public facilities, and $28 million to homes and businesses.

News of the terrible flooding in Buffalo reached President Kennedy, who was on Cape Cod after the premature birth of his son Patrick, who later died. The president dispatched federal officials to inspect, and assess the damage. He ultimately declared the area a federal disaster. This enabled homeowners and businesses to take out low interest loans to help repair the damage.

# Wartime in Western New York

Transportation and wartime production came to a halt in the middle of December of 1944. A furious snowstorm battered the East Coast and affected the Buffalo area! Some parts of New York State were hit by over 20 inches of snow.

Call it lucky if you will, but Buffalo received 13 inches of the heavy white stuff, with gale force winds. This crippling storm claimed five lives in our area alone, and forced the closing of all schools and businesses for days.

Buffalo was the hub of war production, and thousands of tons of war material was stranded in freight yards. Yard operations were tangled despite efforts of crews of snow shovelers to keep switches open. Train traffic was halted as people who lived on the East Coast tried to dig out.

Soldiers of the Second Service Command were put into service to help the city return to normal. The order to help Buffalo dig out was given by Col. John M. McDowell, commanding officer of the Western New York Military District. His orders brought out huge wreckers, heavy trucks with plenty of heavy chains to assist stuck motorists.

Leg power was how the common man got about the city, as bus and trolley service was severely curtailed. "Will open as soon as possible" was a familiar sign spotted in many downtown stores as employees arrived hours late for work or failed to put in an appearance at all.

This storm didn't distract horse race betters. Buffalo Police raided an establishment at 62 East Chippewa St. There were more than 50 people who were chased out of this illegal betting parlor, with three arrests. Police seized telephones, and racing sheets and betting slips.

# Post War Blizzard Buries the City and Steel Plants Shut Down

The city and its southern suburbs were held in winter's snowy grip during the second week of December 1945. Buffalo Mayor Joseph Kelly proclaimed a state of emergency as the city was slammed by a series of "Blizzard" like snowstorms of the "lake effect" variety in less than a week.

It paralyzed street car and bus service, closed schools, closed the airport due to zero visibility, and forced Republic and Bethlehem Steel to shut down operations. Two men died from heart attacks shoveling snow, and two others were stricken.

1,200 workers at Bethlehem Steel were given cots to sleep on after working 30 hour shifts at a time. Officials at Bethlehem were hopeful that production could be kept up, but sidings and switches ended up being frozen. The inclement weather forced the plant to shut down.

Lackawanna's total snowfall was 68 inches of well-packed snow and Lancaster's was 71 inches. The Tonawandas and other Northern suburbs received very little snow. Because the snow depth was so high, Syracuse, Erie Pennsylvania, and Toronto sent snow fighting equipment to help Buffalo and Southern communities battle the elements. At one time there were 115 plows stubbornly fighting to keep roads open in the area.

Mayor Kelly contacted Washington officials to release surplus military goods to be used for the emergency. At the request of the mayor, Gov. Dewey ordered the Motor Transport Co. and Scout Car Platoon of the Fourth Brigade New York Guard into service. Their duty was to help free the streets of illegally parked, and abandoned cars.

# The Perseid Meteor Shower

Every year during the second week of August, the heavens treat the Northeast to a spectacular celestial fireworks display known as, "The Perseid Meteor Shower." This annual event has been observed since the Middle Ages.

This recurring phenomena can be observed well after midnight in the Northeastern sky. These displays are most visible when there is a clear sky, and there is no full moon. At times you can see a meteor a minute, up to sixty an hour. Some have christened this phenomenon the "Tears Of St. Lawrence."

There was a belief among Catholics who lived in parts of England and Germany that the burning tears of St. Lawrence were seen in the sky on the night of August 10, the anniversary of his martyrdom.

St. Lawrence was tortured and killed in Rome on August 10, 258, during the reign of the anti-Christian emperor Valerian. The peasants in Europe believe that St. Lawrence weeps tears of fire which fall from the sky every year of his fete. (the 10th of August)

# The Year Without a Summer

Can you imagine a year without a summer? Well it did happen in 1816. The unusual weather began in May of that year and continued until September covering all the Northeast and adjoining provinces of Canada. Flowers did not bloom until very late, if at all, and many fruit trees did not open their blossoms until the end of May. A few days later a killing of frost occurred, destroying corn and other veggies.

Finally the days warmed in early June, and farmers set out to plant, but a blast of cold air was ready to bring more setbacks. In fact, it was so cold that thousands of birds froze to death and there were two snow falls. June 6 saw snow fall in Western and Northern New York, Vermont, Maine and New Hampshire. The Catskill Mountains saw snow on June 7 and 8.

Actually the years from 1812 to 1817 were considered cold over the entire earth. Weather scientist, William Humphreys wrote a hundred years later that the cold years were caused by dust from a volcano that shielded the earth from the sun's rays. But alas, the poor farmers of 1816 knew nothing about what caused that dreadful summer . . . and by the way the following winter was so cold, mercury froze in thermometers. Residents must have thought the world was coming to an end and the sun was burning itself out.

# Indian Summer

One of the most controversial weather questions could be summed-up this way: "Just when is Indian Summer?"

I've had many discussions with viewers on this matter. Many folks believe that Indian Summer can occur after the first frost. Incidentally, Indian Summer means a few days of pleasant warmth with sunny skies.

Let's set the record straight once and for all. Indian Summer happens only after the first snowfall. The legend goes as follows: during the frontier wars, early settlers and back-woodsmen enjoyed no peace except during the winter months, when Indians were unable to make visits upon settler's land. For this reason, winter was looked upon as a time of great joy.

These early inhabitants had been forced to stay indoors through the fall. With the arrival of winter and its snow, they returned to their farms and cabins to do the jobs that needed to be done before the full fury of winter set in. Crops had to be harvested, animals fattened, roofs repaired. With the arrival of warmer weather, the snow would start to melt and the air filled with a visible haze. If conditions prevailed for several days, it was called Indian Summer.

# Weather Service Office Notes

These notes prior to 1949 were copied from the records of the station. They were originally written by the various Buffalo observers or meteorologists stationed here. For nearly 75 years, the National Weather Service Office in Buffalo was located Downtown overlooking the waterfront.

From first opening on November 1, 1870, the office was located in the Brown Building on Main and Seneca Streets. It was moved on August 31, 1871 to the Weed Block at Main and Swan Streets. The office remained at that location for over ten years, when it was moved into the White Building at the same intersection.

In 1883, the office was once again moved, to the Board of Trade Building at Seneca and Pearl Streets. From March 1, 1896 through February 13, 1913, the Weather Bureau Office was located in the Guaranty (Prudential) Building at Church and Pearl Streets. The final downtown location was at Church and Franklin Streets in the New York Telephone Building from 1913 to 1943.

In June of 1943, Greater Buffalo International Airport became the official location of the office. Observations there were taken at the Administration Building through August of 1960 at which time the Weather Bureau Observatory was completed at the East end of the airport.

Weather notes after 1948 were written from station records, reports and newspaper clippings.

**Persons in Charge of the Weather Office — Buffalo, New York**
October 12, 1870 - October 31, 1870 — William F. Slater
November 1, 1870 - December 31, 1925 — David Cuthbertson
January 1, 1926 - July 31, 1940 — James H. Spencer
August 1, 1940 - March 31, 1942 — Ralph C. Mize
April 1, 1942 - November 19, 1942 — Andrew P. Keller
November 20, 1942 - June 7, 1947 — William H. Tracey
June 8, 1945 - December 30, 1965 — Bernard L. Wiggin
December 31, 1965 - April 5, 1966 — Benjamin Kolker
April 6, 1967 - February 25, 1977 — James E. Smith
February 26, 1977 - July 3, 1977 — Benjamin Kolker
July 4, 1977 - September 3, 1993 — Donald E. Wuerch
August 1993 - Present — Guy E. Tucker

# January 11

## 1905

**Rain and Sleet** — The rain which began at 6:50 p.m. froze as it fell. By 8 p.m., it formed a crust on the snow from one eighth to a quarter of an inch thick, and a solid sheet of ice on the sidewalks which rendered conditions under foot the most precarious thus far of the season. People were falling constantly, unable to keep their footing, the ice was so smooth and slippery. On the streets where the snow was packed down by heavy travel, the conditions were nearly as bad, and many dangerous falls to pedestrians occurred.

## 1980

**Heavy Rains** — 0.86 inch of rain fell at the Buffalo Airport. The heavy rain was accompanied by high winds which caused power outages to Amherst, Buffalo, Dunkirk, and Grand Island, affecting nearly 7,000 residences. There was renewed flooding along the shoreline of Lake Erie. Route 5 near Athol Springs was closed by the high water levels. With subfreezing temperatures at night, the crashing waves created a thick coat of ice on nearby power lines, trees, and houses.

## 1982

**Near Blizzard** — An outbreak of arctic air on the 10th and 11th led to a heavy lake effect snowstorm that paralyzed a 40 mile wide area from Buffalo to Rochester. Hundreds of people were stranded during the storm as high winds and snow combined to produce near zero visibilities and heavy drifting. Two people stranded in their cars froze to death. The storm was promptly named the Blizzard of '82. Conditions were similar to the Blizzard of '77 but this storm didn't last nearly as long and the winds were not as strong. The storm broke a 24 hour snowfall record with 25.3 inches on the 10th and 11th, but the depths were never excessive due to the compacting effect of the wind.

# January 21

## 1906

**High Temperature** — No ice in the harbor during the past week. This is the warmest day in January on record, up to date, at this station. A maximum of 69 degrees from 3 to 5 p.m.

Joe Traver

## 1985

**Blizzard of '85** — January 19th - 22nd — Special weather statements were issued beginning Thursday the 17th warning of the wintry week-end upcoming. Friday afternoon the first winter storm watch for Saturday was posted. That evening the watch was changed to a winter storm warning for high winds, blowing and drifting snow, localized snow squalls, and extreme cold associated with deep low pressure approaching from the midwest. Winter storm warnings remained in effect until Monday morning when blizzard warnings were posted.

Saturday, January 19th: a snow squall off Lake Erie extended through Metropolitan Buffalo and Erie, Wyoming, Genesee, Orleans, and part of Monroe counties. Winds gusted over 40 mph and blizzard like conditions prevailed in the squall. A total of 15.6 inches of snow fell at Buffalo Airport with other areas reporting higher amounts. The high for the day was 26 degrees at 1 a.m. and the low at 10 p.m. was 8 degrees.

Sunday January 20th: Snow squalls moved south to "traditional" snow belts, however, strong winds with gusts to 50 mph and temperatures in the single digits created treacherous conditions throughout the day. Most roads in Erie County were open because of round-the-clock plowing, but whiteouts were making them impossible at times. States of Emergency were declared in Niagara and Orleans Counties. The New York State Thruway closed from the Pennsylvania line to Utica. An additional 2.7 inches of snow fell. High for the day was 11 degrees at midnight; the low was –1 at 9:30 p.m.

Monday January 21st: The storm reached blizzard proportions. Western New York was paralyzed and a driving ban instituted for the city of Buffalo and the five Western New York counties. All schools, factories, and offices were closed. Amtrak service, the Buffalo Airport, and Metro Bus Lines shut down. Winds, gusting over 50 mph, and temperatures about or below zero held wind chills to 50 to 60 degrees below zero a better part of the day. An additional 14.9 inches of snow was reported at the airport. A record low of –10 degrees was set at 4:30 a.m. breaking the previous record of –7 degrees set in 1924.

Tuesday January 22nd: Temperatures rose into the 20s and winds began slowly subsiding. Another 1.2 inches of snow fell at the Buffalo Airport. The four day storm snow total was 34.4 inches accompanied by frequent whiteouts, winds gusting over 50 mph, and up to eight foot snow drifts. Governor Cuomo declared Erie, Niagara, Orleans, Genesee, and Wyoming counties disaster areas. Mayor Griffin banned driving in the City of Buffalo until Friday the 25th. Five deaths were related to the storm, two from exposure. Schools in the area were closed for the entire week.

# January 27

## 1974

**Windstorm** — Peak gust of 66 mph. Average velocity for the day 28.4 mph. Widespread damage was reported. A 70-foot radio tower in Hamburg was blown down and a 50-foot beacon demolished at Perry/Warsaw Airport. In Albion, a roof was blown off an apartment building and a mobile home overturned. Lake Shore Road in the town of Hamburg was closed due to spray from Lake Erie on the road.

## 1985

**Niagara River Ice Jam** — January 26th-27th — A massive ice jam, blamed on the Blizzard of '85 clogged the entire east channel of the Niagara River. The fragile Lake Erie ice cover caused by warmer than usual temperatures was broken up and moved downriver by the extreme southwest winds of the Blizzard. The ice then solidified and jammed up as it moved into the narrow and shallow east channel. Damage was reported to boat hoists, piers, and the ricer banks as well as houses on both sides of the river.

**Store Roof Collapse** — A large section of a store roof collapsed in the Clarence Mall, injuring nine persons. The roof collapsed due to the excessive weight of snow from the blizzard. Along with 10-foot deep snow, heavy girders and a commercial air conditioning unit fell to the floor. Over a dozen ambulances, three helicopters, and five volunteer fire companies were called to the scene. The store had just opened for the day reportedly resulting in the low number of injuries.

# January 28

## 1926

**Low Temperature Storm** — The temperature fell from 23 degrees at midnight of the 27th to minus 2 degrees at 6 a.m. of the 29th. On the 28th, Buffalo was swept by a 56 mph gale swept from the streets everything movable and piled high the snow which had fallen during the night. At 3 p.m. the gale had subsided to 46 mph and gradually diminished from that point. Many of the streets were made impassable by the storm. The worst effect was felt on the Hamburg Turnpike.

# 1968

**Heavy Fog** — January 28th-30th — Periods of heavy fog hampered highway and air travel. The airport was closed from 10 a.m. of the 29th with visibilities ranging from near zero to 1/4 mile for the 24 hour period.

# 1977

**Blizzard of '77** — January 28th - February 1st — Snow began falling in Buffalo about 5 a.m. of the 28th. As winds freshened from the south ahead of a sharpening front, about two inches of new powder had accumulated on top of the 37 inch snowpack and drifts from previous storms dating back to Christmas. City streets were already clogged so badly that the National Guard was called in even before anyone knew about the coming blizzard. During the morning the temperature rose rapidly from 5 degrees at midnight to 26 degrees at 11 a.m. At 11:35 a.m., the front passed Buffalo Airport. In a short time the visibility dropped from 3/4 of a mile to zero in just over four hours. The blizzard reached its worst severity during the late afternoon as winds at the airport averaged 46 mph gusting to 69 mph. Gusts of 75 mph were recorded at Niagara Falls Airport. An average speed of 46 mph and temperature of minus 1 degree resulted in a wind chill factor of 55 to 60 degrees below zero which probably contributed to the deaths of 29 people — many found frozen in their half buried cars during the four day ordeal. Blizzard or near blizzard conditions prevailed on and off for the next three days ending about midday February 1st. Daily peak gusts of 51, 52, 58, and 46 mph were recorded on the 29th through the 1st. When the sun finally came out for good on the first of February, its cold light revealed a scene of incredible desolation in the Buffalo area and to a slightly lesser degree in much of the seven Western County area. The city as well as most other communities banned traffic for several days. The Army was called in from Fort Bragg, N.C. to augment the number of National Guard Troops which had been called before the storm. Some of the eastern suburbs of Buffalo, particularly Lancaster, were buried — to the roof in some cases. President Carter declared seven western counties and two eastern Lake Ontario counties a federal disaster area — the first time ever for a snowstorm in the U.S. The snow at Buffalo Airport totaled about 12 inches from January 28th to February 1st but much of this is believed to be from existing snow lying on the frozen surface of Lake Erie being blown into the Buffalo area and redeposited.

# 1986

**Whiteouts** — Whiteout conditions on the Father Baker Bridge caused an approximately 40 car pile-up that forced authorities to temporarily close the Father Baker Bridge and the Skyway in both directions. While no serious injuries were reported, police said some persons were taken to area hospitals.

# Groundhog Day

The highest temperature ever recorded on Ground Hog Day was 57 degrees in 1973. The lowest ever was minus 20 in 1961. Normally, the high averages about 28 degrees and the low temperature around 15.

There is just over an 85 percent chance of having precipitation of a trace or more most likely snow. The greatest amount of precipitation recorded was 0.75 inch in 1892. The most snowfall was 4.4 inches in 1912.

If the groundhog lived in Buffalo instead of Punxsutawney, he only would have seen his shadow ten times in the past 100 years.

In 1904, a veritable blizzard raged throughout the day. Light snow began early in the morning and continued until midnight. The loose dry snow was blown about and drifted by a wind of 32 to 47 mph.

A windstorm in 1907 raised the water in harbor several feet and the ice at this end of the Lake was considerably broken up. Many wires were broken down causing delay in telegraph and telephone service and putting out the lights. Many showcases and signs were blown down and windows broken.

Snowmelt and about 1½ inches of rain caused ice jams and caused localized flooding along Cazenovia Creek in 1970. In West Seneca, 30 families had to be evacuated in that area of the creek.

High winds again caused problems in 1981 and 1983. In 1981, winds gusted over 50 mph. Blowing snow and heavy squalls south of Buffalo caused many minor traffic accidents and traffic jams. The Thruway was closed by nearly two feet of snow near the Pennsylvania State Line. In 1983, wind gusts over 70 mph occurred in Chautauqua County. They knocked out electric power to more than 1,000 customers and flipped over two tractor trailer units parked along the Thruway.

# February 26

## 1887

**Gale** — Severe gale set in at 12:40 p.m. continuing until after midnight. It proceeded to be the most destructive known here for years. Six houses in the course of construction were leveled to the ground. The house on Ferry Street in falling crushed to death Detective Captain James Shepard. A large number of ladies returning from places of amusement were hurt. The streets were completely strewn with signs, trees, telegraph lines and billboards. A number of show windows and cases suffered from the gale. Ice on the lake was broken up into large fields by the high wind. It was reported that a number of fishermen were on the ice. The gale continued throughout the entire next day reaching a maximum of 48 mph. Snow fell the entire day. On the 28th a search party found the bodies of two men from this city who had been caught up in the break up of the ice.

## 1936

**Flood Conditions** — On the 26th, as a result of several days of warm weather and the rapid melting of snow and ice, streams in Western New York became swollen. At East Aurora, the overflow of Cazenovia Creek caused about $4000 damage to the legion hall. Some cellars in South Buffalo were flooded by the high water from the creek.

## 1946

**Sleet and Freezing Rain** — Sleet and freezing rain and drizzle caused glazed highways impeding traffic. One half an inch of sleet fell during the day. Air traffic was temporarily suspended by icing conditions.

## 1975

**Near Record Warmth** (high temperature of 58 degrees) was accompanied by high winds and thunderstorms. A small tornado touched down on Five Mile Road in Allegany County. Five mobile homes were destroyed and six damaged.

## 1932

**Warm Spell** — February 1932 — This was the 14th consecutive month that the monthly mean temperature has been above normal. The meteorological winter (December, January, and February) had an average temperature of 34.7 degrees, this being the warmest winter on record at this station; the previous was 33.9 degrees in 1889-1890.

# 1936

**Ice formation at Niagara Falls and Lower River** — January-February 1936. The persistent cold weather caused the worst ice blockade of recent years at Niagara Falls. By January 25th, the flow of water over the American Falls had practically disappeared. Many sections of the American channel were characterized by congested ice hummocks, forming a bridge of ice. The jam in the Lower River at Lewiston extended from above the Queenston Ontario plant of the Ontario Hydro Plant to the River's mouth, a distance of approximately six miles. The height of some ice formations in this section were estimated at 4 feet. This ice jam grew worse from day to day, and finally resulted in early February in a property loss estimated at $30,000 or more. Boat houses, cottages, the docks at Kingston, etc. along the banks of the river were damaged or destroyed by the rising ice and water. During three weeks or more, beginning about January 19th, tens of thousands of people were attracted to Niagara Falls and the Lower Bridge to view these exceptional conditions. The ice formations were magnificent. Due to warmer weather, the ice bridge, the jam in the Lower River, etc. showed signs of breaking up during the last week of February.

# 1984

**Leap Year Snowstorm** — February 27th - 29th — An intense low pressure system which developed over the Central Plains brought over two feet of snow and strong gusty winds to Western New York. The first statement issued by the National Weather Service released during the afternoon of Sunday, February 26th headlined more wintry weather headed for Western New York. Early Monday morning — February 27th — a winter storm watch was posted for all of Western and Central New York. Later that afternoon the watch was upgraded to a warning. Snow began falling at the Buffalo Airport about 5:30 p.m. on the 27th and before ending on the 29th, 28.3 inches had fallen. Reports received from throughout Western New York ranged from one to three feet. The Niagara Falls-North Tonawanda areas being the hardest hit. Travel was almost completely stopped. A state-of-emergency was declared in Niagara County prohibiting all travel. Virtually all area schools and businesses were closed on the 28th and 29th. Buffalo International Airport was closed for 36 hours as crews were unable to keep runways clear for safe landings and takeoffs.

Northwest winds averaging about 20 miles an hour and gusts about 35 mph caused blowing and drifting snow reducing visibilities to near zero at times. Eight deaths were attributed to the storm including the deaths of two sisters due to carbon monoxide poisoning when their car became stranded in a snowbank.

A number of records were broken by the storm including the maximum snowfall in a 24 hour period for the month of February: 19.4 inches fell from Monday evening through Tuesday evening. The old record of 16.1 inches set February 10th and 11th, 1910 was easily surpassed. It was the 5th largest 24 hour snowfall total for Buffalo. Snowfall of 4.2 inches on the 27th tied the record for maximum snowfall for that date and snowfall of 18.4 inches and 5.7 inches on the 28th and 29th, respectively set new records for those dates, melted snow of 1.74 inches set the record for maximum precipitation ever recorded on February 28th.

# St. Patrick's Day – March 17

The highest temperature ever recorded in Buffalo on St. Patrick's Day was 69 degrees in 1945. The lowest temperature was recorded in 1967 when the mercury dipped to minus four degrees. Normally, the high averages around 38 degrees and the low near 24.

There has been precipitation of a trace or more on 75 of the past 98 St. Patrick's Days. In 1936, a severe snow storm dumped 19.0 inches of snow on Buffalo — the most ever for the date. The melted snow yielded 2.62 inches of water — setting the record for the precipitation for March 17th. Nearly 300 tons of water per acre fell in the storm. So deep and heavy was the snow that by mid-afternoon street car service ceased. Also, conditions became indescribably bad for auto, bus, and other traffic. Total losses resulting from the storm are difficult to determine. Actual property loss was perhaps $100,000 including collapse of buildings, damage to many automobiles, etc. Extra funds for cleaning streets and removing snow were $175,000. The International Railway Company was hard hit due to the loss of business and the heavy expense incidental to its efforts to keep the street cat lines running, and then to reopen them up after a complete shutdown occurred. Interference with business due to the terrible street conditions caused the merchants severe loss of business.

In 1935, a severe wind storm passed over the city. Damage was chiefly of a minor nature. A four-story steel framework for the new Kensington High School was twisted and partly flattened by the wind;

a portion of a fire escape was torn from a building on Seneca Street injuring one person; part of the roof of Academy Theater was torn off; several plate glass windows were broken; and a few signs, billboards, and chimneys were blown down. Ferry operations between Tonawanda and Grand Island were suspended part of the morning. The wind was not unusually strong prior to 6 a.m. and died down rapidly after 2 p.m..

As a result of heavy rains in Western New York averaging nearly an inch for the area and high waters due to melting of snow during the past week, many creeks and streams overflowed their banks in 1942. Damage was estimated at $1,000,000. The most damage occurred in counties south of Buffalo, Cattaraugus and Chautauqua in particular. Roads, bridges, and farms were inundated by rampaging waters from swollen creeks and streams while hundreds of homes and businesses reported flooded cellars and basements. Thirteen bridges were washed out in Chautauqua County. Lake Chautauqua at Jamestown was 24 inches below its all time high level. Many head of livestock were drowned. Tonawanda Creek at Batavia went 14 feet over its bank. Flood conditions were also quite general near Lancaster and West Seneca.

Local flooding again occurred in 1963. Mild weather caused local flooding from snowmelt and ice jams. Cattaraugus Creek overflowed at Sunset Bay causing extensive damage to many homes. There was lesser flooding on other streams. High temperature, reaching 59 degrees, and considerable morning sunshine contributed to the snowmelt.

**Period of record:** 100 years 1890-1989

**Temperature data:** St. Patrick's Day

**Highest:**    69 degrees in 1945
**Lowest:**    −4 degrees in 1967

**Lowest maximum:**       4 degrees in 1885
**Highest maximum:**    49 degrees in 1919

**Average high temperature:**    38.1 degrees
**Average low temperature:**    24.2 degrees

**High temperature by 10 degree ranges:**

| Teens | 20s | 30s | 40s | 50s | 60s | |
|-------|-----|-----|-----|-----|-----|---|
| 4 | 14 | 46 | 21 | 9 | 6 | Number of |
| 4% | 14% | 46% | 21% | 9% | 6% | occurrences |

**Precipitation data:**

Number of times with measurable precipitation       55 or 55%
Number of times with a trace or more precipitation   77 or 77%
Number of times with no precipitation               23 or 23%

**Snowfall:**  Number of times with a trace or more      58
Number of times with over a trace       34
Number of times with 1.0 inch or more   10
Number of times with 5.0 inches or more   2

**Maximum precipitation:**  2.62 inches in 1936

**Maximum snowfall:**       19.0 inches in 1936

# Easter Sunday

The warmest Easter occurred on April 18, 1976 when the high temperature reached 81 degrees. The lowest temperature ever recorded on Easter was five degrees on April 1, 1923.

There is roughly a 60 percent chance of having precipitation of a trace or more. The most precipitation ever recorded on an Easter Sunday was 0.91 inch on April 3. 1988. The most snow on an Easter was 1.0 inch on April 11, 1982 and April 2, 1961.

On Easter in 1912, April 7th, a wind storm drove the ice into the entrance of the inner harbor and up the creek forcing large fields of ice down the river. The gale loosened the anchorage of the large steamers and forced them into shallow water.

On Easter 1974, April 14, a severe thunderstorm swept across Chautauqua County. A small tornado touched down in French Creek but only minor damage was reported.

**Period of record:** 116 years 1874-1989

**Temperature data:** Easter Sunday

**Highest temperature:**   81 degrees on April 18, 1976
**Lowest temperature:**    5 degrees on April 1, 1923

**Lowest maximum:**   20 degrees on March 24, 1940
**Highest maximum:**  55 degrees on March 17, 1938, March 18, 1976

**Precipitation data:**

Number of times with measurable precipitation            48 or 42%
Number of times with a trace or more precipitation      70 or 61%
Number of times with no precipitation                           46 or 40%

**Maximum precipitation:**  0.91 inches on April 3, 1988

**Maximum snowfall:** 1.0 inch on April 11, 1982 and April 2, 1961

**Further data on the 15 most recent Easters (1975-1989)**

**Temperature data:**

**High temperatures have been:**
50 degrees or more — 9 out of last 15 years
60 degrees or more — 5 out of last 15 years
70 degrees or more — 3 out of last 15 years
80 degrees or more — 1 out of last 15 years

**Precipitation data:**

There has been precipitation (trace or more) 8 out of the last 15 years.

It has snowed on 2 out the last 15 Easters:
    March 30, 1975 & April 11, 1982

The coldest in the past 15 years:
    March 20, 1975 — High 35, Low 23 (0.7 inch of snow)

The warmest in the past 15 years:
    April 18, 1976 — High 81, Low 55 (no precipitation)

# April 22

## 1985

**Record Temperatures — Warm Spell** — April 22nd - 23rd. A high temperature of 77 degrees on the 22nd broke the record of 76 set in 1957 and 1973. The high of 88 degrees on the 23rd not only broke a 100 year record for that date, but also set a new record for the highest temperature ever recorded on any date during the month of April. Many trees and flowers started to bud early due to the warm days and fairly mild nights which occurred during the latter part of the month. This also enabled farmers to get an early start plowing fields and readying them for spring planting.

# May 2

## 1884

**Severe Gale** — The most severe gale experienced since the opening of navigation. The gale commenced at 4:30 a.m. continuing to increase in velocity until 10:15 a.m. when it reached 46 mph and between 10 and 11 a.m. was steady at 40 mph for the entire hour. Gale ended at 4:45 p.m. Upwards of fifty vessels were delayed by the gale and steamers arriving from other ports were unable to reach Buffalo as the ice was packed solid in the mouth and for 600 yards out into the lake. A schooner was driven on the reefs remaining there for two days when she was taken off by tug boats. A two story house was blown over but no one was hurt. One man was drowned having fallen out a small boat and was covered with ice which had been driven rapidly by high winds. A large number of chimneys, fences, signs, trees, and cornices suffered from the gale. Also, moving wagons were turned over and contents destroyed.

## 1972

**Tornado** — A tornado struck South Wales/Varysburg area during the evening.

## 1983

**Tornado** — One of the worst tornadoes in Western New York history raked parts of Chautauqua County killing two people and critically injuring four others. Damage estimates were over 3 million dollars. The worst damage was reported at the Chautauqua Shores Housing Development on the borders of the Chautauqua Institution. Winds downed 480 utility poles, blacking out 4,250 homes. Winds also damaged about 10 homes on the Chautauqua Institution grounds and demolished the facility's small yacht club, as well as downing 25 trees on the adjoining golf course.

# May 21

## 1980

**Volcanic Ash** — Volcanic ash from Mt. St. Helens in the state of Washington reached Buffalo on this date. It was a barely discernible high haze layer in the day which enhanced the colors of the sunset.

# Mother's Day

The highest temperature ever recorded on Mother's Day was 83 degrees on May 14, 1961. The lowest temperature recorded on May 12, 1963 when the mercury dropped to 32 degrees. Normally, the high averages about 62 degrees and the low near 45.

The most precipitation ever recorded on Mother's Day was 1.11 inches on May 12, 1974. It has snowed on four . . . the most being 0.5 inch on May 8, 1977.

Thunderstorms have occurred on five occasions.

**Period of record:** 78 years 1912-1989

**Temperature data:** Mother's Day

**Highest:**    83 degrees on May 14, 1961 & May 12, 1985
**Lowest:**     32 degrees on May 12, 1963

**Lowest maximum:**     42 degrees on May 13, 1923
**Highest maximum:**    66 degrees on May 10, 1966 & May 9, 1965

**Average high temperature:**    61.7 degrees
**Average low temperature:**     44.8 degrees

**High temperature by 10 degree ranges:**

| 40s | 50s | 60s | 70s | 80s | |
|-----|-----|-----|-----|-----|--|
| 9 | 27 | 19 | 19 | 4 | Number of occurrences |
| 12% | 35% | 25% | 25% | 6% | |

**Precipitation data:**

| | |
|---|---|
| Number of times with measurable precipitation | 34 or 44% |
| Number of times with a trace or more precipitation | 49 or 63% |
| Number of times with no precipitation | 29 or 38% |

**Thunderstorms occurred on 5 occasions:**
1912, 1918. 1932, 1956, 1959

**Snow occurred on 4 occasions:** 0.5 inch on May 8, 1977
Trace on May 8, 1955; May 8, 1963; May 13, 1984

**Precipitation of:**    0.01 or more    34 occurrences
                         0.50 or more    6 occurrences
                         1.00 or more    2 occurrences

**Maximum precipitation:**  1.11 inches on May 12, 1974

# Memorial Day

Traditionally, Memorial Day was observed May 30th. Since the Monday Holiday Bill, it is observed on the last Monday in May.

The warmest Memorial Day occurred May 30, 1944 when a high temperature of 87 degrees was recorded. The record low temperature of 34 degrees was set May 30, 1961. Normally, the high averages near 68 degrees and the low temperature averages around 50.

There is roughly a 45 percent chance of having precipitation of a trace or more. The most rain received on Memorial Day was 1.14 inches on May 30, 1880.

**Period of record:** 116 years 1874-1989

**Temperature data:** Memorial Day

**Highest:**    87 degrees on May 30, 1944
**Lowest:**    34 degrees on May 30, 1961

**Lowest maximum:**    51 degrees on May 30, 1930
**Highest maximum:**    66 degrees on May 29, 1978

**Average high temperature:**    67.9 degrees
**Average low temperature:**    50.5 degrees

### High temperature by 10 degree ranges:

| 50s | 60s | 70s | 80s | |
|-----|-----|-----|-----|-----|
| 27 | 33 | 40 | 15 | Number of occurrences |
| 24% | 29% | 35% | 13% | |

**Precipitation data:**

| | |
|---|---|
| Number of times with measurable precipitation | 34 or 28% |
| Number of times with a trace or more precipitation | 52 or 45% |
| Number of times with no precipitation | 62 or 54% |

**Precipitation of:**    0.01 or more    32 occurrences
0.50 or more    5 occurrences
1.00 or more    2 occurrences

**Maximum precipitation:**  1.14 inches on May 30, 1980

# Father's Day

The highest temperature ever recorded on Father's Day was 93 degrees on June 21, 1953. The lowest ever recorded occurred on June 18, 1950 when the mercury dropped to 40 degrees. Normally, the high temperature averages near 74 degrees and the low about 58.

There is roughly a 50 percent chance of having precipitation of a trace or more and thunderstorms have occurred on 8 of the past 75 father's days. The most precipitation ever recorded was 1.05 inches on June 17, 1984. Moderate to heavy rain fell over the entire Western New York area. Rainfall amounts of over three inches occurred in Chautauqua and Erie Counties. Many small streams overflowed their banks and Chautauqua Lake was above flood stage. In Chautauqua County, five bridges were washed out.

**Period of record:** 80 years 1910-1989

**Temperature data:** 3rd Sunday in June

**Highest:**    93 degrees on June 21, 1953
**Lowest:**     40 degrees on June 18, 1930

**Lowest maximum:**      56 degrees on June 15, 1969
**Highest maximum:**     71 degrees on June 15, 1950

**Average high temperature:**    74.5 degrees
**Average low temperature:**     57.4 degrees

**High temperature by 10 degree ranges:**

| 50s | 60s | 70s | 80s | 90s | |
|-----|-----|-----|-----|-----|---|
| 3 | 20 | 31 | 24 | 1 | Number of occurrences |
| 4% | 25% | 40% | 30% | 1% | |

**Precipitation data:**

Number of times with measurable precipitation          29 or 37%
Number of times with a trace or more precipitation     39 or 49%
Number of times with no precipitation                  40 or 50%

**Thunderstorms occurred on 10 occasions:**
1912, 1913, 1937, 1944, 1971, 1974, 1975, 1981, 1985, 1989

**Precipitation of:**   0.01 or more     29 occurrences
                        0.50 or more      5 occurrences
                        1.00 or more      1 occurrences

**Maximum precipitation:**  1.05 inches on June 17, 1984

# June 22

## 1951

**Heavy Thunderstorms** — Heavy thunderstorms caused local flash floods throughout Western New York. Over an inch and a quarter of rain (1.29 inches) fell in 24 hours with 0.90 inch being recorded between 10 p.m. and midnight.

## 1985

**High Winds** — Strong southwest winds on Lake Erie — gusting to 41 mph — claimed one life, capsized several small vessels, and left two teenage girls stranded. A 16-foot fiberglass boat capsized just outside the breakwater of the Erie Basin Marina spilling all four occupants into the water and resulting in the drowning of one. Two teenage girls were stranded adrift a rubber raft for 16 hours about four miles west of Silver Creek before being rescued by the Coast Guard.

## 1987

**Record Rainfall and Floods** — A rainfall total of 5.01 inches on the 22nd shattered the previous record for that date and set a new 24-hour rainfall record. The resulting flooding closed main arteries such as the N.Y.S. Thruway, the Scajaquada Expressway and the Kensington Expressway. The gauge at Scajaquada Creek recorded its highest reading ever — over 5 feet above flood stage. Cheektowaga, Depew and Lancaster suffered the brunt of the suburban flooding. In the City of Buffalo, flooding was reported throughout North Buffalo and the Black Rock section of the city. In North Buffalo, underground telephone cables became water logged and over 100 customers lost phone service. With innumerable streets closed, even normal short commutes home from work took hours.

# Fourth of July

The highest temperature ever recorded on Fourth of July was 92 degrees set in 1988. The lowest ever recorded occurred in 1927 when the mercury dipped to 46 degrees. Normally, the high temperature averages around 77 degrees and the low near 61.

There is roughly a 50 percent chance of having precipitation of a trace or more and thunderstorms have occurred on 25 or the past

115 July Fourths. The most precipitation ever recorded was 1.22 inches in 1871.

A severe thunderstorm occurred in 1900, from 6:30 p.m. to 8 p.m. being intense. Several places were struck by lightening although the damage was mostly minor. The storm was most severe in the northern part of the city where the drops were as large as marbles.

**Period of record:** 116 years 1874-1989

**Temperature data:** Fourth of July

**Highest:**    92 degrees in 1988
**Lowest:**    46 degrees in 1927

**Lowest maximum:**    63 degrees in 1882
**Highest maximum:**    78 degrees in 1897

**Average high temperature:**    77.4 degrees
**Average low temperature:**    60.9 degrees

**High temperature by 10 degree ranges:**

| 60s | 70s | 80s | 90s | |
|-----|-----|-----|-----|--|
| 16 | 54 | 41 | 5 | Number of occurrences |
| 14% | 47% | 36% | 5% | |

**Precipitation data:**

Number of times with measurable precipitation    48 or 42%
Number of times with a trace or more precipitation    55 or 48%
Number of times with no precipitation    61 or 52%

**Number of days With precipitation of:**    0.01 inch or more  48
0.50 inch or more    8
1.00 inch or more    2

Thunderstorms have occurred on 25 or the past 116 July 4th's (or 22%)

**Maximum precipitation:**   1.22 inches in 1871

**Number of days:**    Cloudy    17 or 15%
Partly cloudy    69 or 60%
Clear    29 or 25%

# July 25

## 1987

**Record Lake Erie Water Temperature** — The Lake Erie water temperature at Buffalo rose to 79 degrees on the 25th and 26th — the warmest since records began in 1926. The previous record was 78 degrees set August 10, 11, & 12, 1949.

# Labor Day

Labor Day is observed on the first Monday in September. Labor Day was first celebrated in New York in 1882 under the sponsorship of the Central Labor Union. The idea was suggested by Peter J. McGuire, of the Knights of Labor, that the day be set aside in honor of labor.

The highest temperature ever recorded in Buffalo on Labor Day was on September 7, 1959 when bright, sunny skies were accompanied by a high temperature of 89 degrees. On the other side of the spectrum, clear skies during the early morning hours of September 6, 1976 resulted in a record low temperature of 43 degrees. Normally, the high temperature averaged near 76 degrees while the low averages about 60.

There is roughly a 50 percent chance of having at least a trace of precipitation and about a 20 percent chance of a thunderstorm. On September 1, 1980 afternoon thunderstorms dropped 1.26 inches of rain at the Buffalo Airport — the most precipitation ever recorded on a Labor Day.

On Labor Day in 1944 — September 4th — a moderate earthquake was felt at 11:39 p.m. The quake was centered about 300 miles northeast of Buffalo. Perceptible vibrations were felt in homes and buildings. Light furniture was displaced and dishes rattled. No damage, however, was reported in the Buffalo area. The shock was felt throughout the northeastern United States and Ontario. Property damage was reported in Ontario.

**Period of record:** 80 years 1910-1989

**Temperature data:** First Monday in September

**Highest:**   89 degrees on September 7, 1959
**Lowest:**    43 degrees on September 6, 1976

**Lowest maximum:**      62 degrees on September 1, 1958
**Highest maximum:**     73 degrees on September 4, 1961

**Average high temperature:**   75.9 degrees
**Average low temperature:**    59.2 degrees

**High temperature by 10 degree ranges:**

| 60s | 70s | 80s | |
|-----|-----|-----|--|
| 14  | 44  | 22  | Number of occurrences |
| 17% | 55% | 27% | |

**Precipitation data:**

Number of times with measurable precipitation     25 or 31%
Number of times with a trace or more precipitation  38 or 47%
Number of times with no precipitation             42 or 52%

**Number of days with precipitation of:**   0.01 inch or more   25
                                            0.50 inch or more    3
                                            1.00 inch or more    2

Thunderstorms have occurred on 14 or the past 80 Labor Days (or 17%)

**Maximum precipitation:**   1.26 inches on September 1, 1980

# Thanksgiving Day

Thanksgiving Day is observed nationally on the fourth Thursday in November. It is believed that the holiday dates back to the Day of Thanks ordered by Governor Bradford of Plymouth Colony in New England in 1621.

The highest temperature ever recorded in Buffalo on Thanksgiving Day was in 1934 when a high of 69 degrees was reached on November 22nd. The lowest temperature ever recorded was 14 degrees on November 26th, 1903. Normally, the high temperature averages 42 degrees and the low about 31 degrees.

There is roughly a 75% chance of a trace or more of precipitation. Rain, sometimes heavy, throughout the day on November 28th, 1968 totaled 0.96 inches . . . the most precipitation ever recorded on a Thanksgiving Day. The most snow that fell on Thanksgiving Day was in 1952 when 10.3 inches was recorded at the airport on November 27th. Most portions of the City of Buffalo received between six and ten inches.

On Thanksgiving Day in 1956, a snowstorm hit from central Erie and Wyoming Counties southward. Four feet of snow was reported from the Springville area. Only a trace of snow was received at the airport and throughout much of Metro Buffalo.

**Period of record:** 100 years 1890-1989

**Temperature data:** Fourth Thursday in November

**Highest:**   68 degrees on November 26, 1896
**Lowest:**    14 degrees on November 26, 1903

**Lowest maximum:**   22 degrees on Nov. 26, 1903 & Nov. 24, 1938
**Highest maximum:**  53 degrees on November 22, 1979

**Average high temperature:**   41.9 degrees
**Average low temperature:**    30.4 degrees

**High temperature by 10 degree ranges:**

| 20s | 30s | 40s | 50s | 60s | |
|-----|-----|-----|-----|-----|--|
| 8 | 36 | 34 | 16 | 6 | Number of occurrences |
| 8% | 36% | 34% | 16% | 6% | Probability of high temp. in that range |

**Precipitation data:**

Number of times with measurable precipitation   54 or 54%
Number of times with a trace or more precipitation   73 or 73%
Number of times with no precipitation   27 or 27%

**Number of days with precipitation of:**  0.01 inch or more   54
0.50 inch or more   7

**Snowfall:** Number of times with a trace or more   44
Number of times with over a trace   26

**Maximum precipitation:**  0.96 inches on November 28, 1968

**Maximum snowfall:**   10.3 inches on November 27, 1952

# Christmas Day

The highest temperature ever recorded on Christmas Day was 64 degrees in 1982. The lowest temperatures occurred two years earlier in 1980 when the mercury dipped to minus 10 degrees. Normally, the high temperature averages near 34 degrees and the low about 22.

The greatest precipitation ever recorded on Christmas Day was 0.94 inch which fell as a mixture of rain and snow in 1974. The most snowfall however was the 6.0 inches which fell on Christmas in 1944.

It has snowed on 80 of the past 117 Christmas Days — and the whitest Christmas was in 1960 when 18 inches of snow was on the ground.

In 1973 on Christmas Day heavy rains caused localized flooding in portions of Western New York. 1.21 inches was recorded at the airport and minor street and basement flooding was reported in Cheektowaga, Tonawanda, and Amherst.

On December 24th, 1978, the ground was bare and brown over most of the Buffalo area and there were golfers spotted at Cazenovia Park. By Christmas morning, several inches of heavy, wet snow had coated everything to create a storybook Christmas setting. Unfortunately, much heavier snowfall amounts east and south of Buffalo played havoc with holiday travelers and stranded motorists.

In 1983 — snowsqualls began over the towns south of Buffalo on December 23rd. Propelled by a west wind, the squalls shifted north to Clarence, Cheektowaga, and some parts of Buffalo, and then south to South Buffalo, Lackawanna, and Hamburg. The airport closed intermittently on the 23rd and 24th and the Thruway was closed from Hamburg to the Pennsylvania line stranding about seven hundred persons. Reported snowfall amounts ranged from 7 to 15 inches.

**Period of record:** 117 years 1873-1989

**Temperature data:** Christmas Day

**Highest:**      64 degrees in 1982
**Lowest:**      –10 degrees in 1980

**Lowest maximum:**      7 degrees in 1983
**Highest maximum:**      55 degrees in 1982

**Warmest Christmas Day:**      1982 — High 64, Low 55, Mean 60
**Coldest Christmas Day:**      1980 — High 16, Low –10, Mean 3

**Average high temperature:**   34.0 degrees
**Average low temperature:**   22.4 degrees

**High temperature by 10 degree ranges:**

| Single Digits | Teens | 20s | 30s | 40s | 50s | 60s | |
|---|---|---|---|---|---|---|---|
| 1 | 8 | 29 | 49 | 21 | 8 | 1 | Number of occurrences |

**Precipitation data:** Since 1884

| | |
|---|---|
| Number of times with 1.0 inch snowfall or more | 20 |
| Number of times with 1.0 inch snowfall or less | 58 |
| Number of times with no snowfall | 29 |

**Snow depth:** Greatest (since 1898) — 18.0 inches in 1960
Over 12":   14 inches in 1916; 13 inches in 1924, 1994, 1983
Over 1":   48 times
Less than 1":   41 times

**Maximum precipitation:**   0.94 inches in 1965 and 1979

**Maximum snowfall:**   6.0 inches in 1944

# December 29

## 1880

**Heavy Snow Storm** — Heavy snow (amount unknown) continued all day without interruption and being accompanied with strong winds produced drifts that have almost entirely stopped railroad and street car travel. Every railroad running into the city has been obliged to extend more than 12 or 15 miles outside of the city. Trade in the city has been seriously interfered with and all travel was suspended through the 30th.

## 1915

**Snow and Sleet** — The heavy snow and sleet (12.2 inches snow, 1.9 inch sleet) greatly impeded street car traffic, the press reporting cars, at least 65, off the tracks in various portions of the city. The snow and sleet packed in the grooved rails and it was necessary to employ several hundred men to clean out rails. At Jewett and Fillmore Avenues, a car crashed into a storefront. Interurban and steam traffic was but little delayed.

## 1933

**Cold Snap** — The temperature fell today to 6.7 degrees below zero shortly after 7:30 a.m. This was the lowest ever recorded on this date, the previous record being 6.0 degrees below zero in 1880. After 1 a.m., the temperature was below zero all day, the average temperature for the day being 3 degrees below zero, also a new December record for Buffalo. One death in Tonawanda was attributed to the cold. There were some cases of frost bite being treated in the hospitals. Many automobiles in the city were stalled during the day, due chiefly to starter and radiator troubles. Train, street car and bus traffic was hampered only moderately. The lake froze over today for the first time this year.

## 1984

**Record Warmth, Heavy Rains, and Localized Flooding** — December 28th-29th — Drizzle began during the afternoon of the 27th. The drizzle became rain on the 28th and amounted to 0.35 inch. Rain continued on the 29th with an additional 1.14 inches being recorded at the airport. Flood warnings were issued on the 29th for Cayuga, Ellicott, Cazenovia, Buffalo and Tonawanda Creeks in Erie County. Area streams crested around a foot to a foot and a half above flood stages. Highway departments and local law enforcement agencies reported some basement flooding and underpass flooding as well as a few road closing. The high temperature of 61 degrees on the 29th broke the old record of 55 degrees set in 1884 and tied in 1889.

# December 31

## 1895

**Snow Squall and High Gale** — December usually the darkest and most dreary of the year went out today in all the majestic splendor of a blizzard, with the exception that the temperature was not as low as usually attends these storms. The day began with rain, the rain continuing until early morning at intervals throughout the entire day, some of the snow squalls being unusually disagreeable and badly drifted, and had the snow been as heavy as expected, much trouble to the small railroads would have resulted. The storm continued throughout the entire day and was one of the most severe storms ever experienced here as far as the steady movement of air is considered.

The wind continued over 40 mph 2 a.m. to 8 p.m. reaching a maximum velocity of 60 mph and at several times during the day it reached 56 mph. The air was filled with signs, boards, fences, and other articles. People who tried to walk the streets were buffeted about and many were blown to the ground. Squaw Island was once more submerged, also strawberry Island and Frog Island at the head of Grand Island and many thousand dollars worth of lumber was carried away by the wind and waves. At 4:33 p.m. the floating elevator belonging to James Ryan broke from its moorings but was recaptured with little damage and a number of canal boats were more or less damaged by high winds and water. The Buffalo creek tracks were useless all day being generally submerged; 600 feet in the southern part of the city suffered in like manner. The buildings of the city stood the blunt of the gale in grand style, when the great fury of the storm is considered giving us an extreme velocity of 73 mph. Casualties were unroofing of part of the Court Street Theater, parts of the corner of the Builders Exchange, and the NYC RR track under water, the embankment being washed out. Ropes were stretched along the street so pedestrians could walk.

# 1985

**Record Monthly Snowfall** — Total snowfall for the month of December set a new record for the month and for any one month at Buffalo.

68.4 inches exceeded the previous record for December of 60.7 inches set in December 1976. The total was 0.1 inch more than the previous record for any month (68.3 inches recorded in January 1977) — a rather misleading statistic as January of 1977 was a much windier, colder and blustery month. Only one daily snowfall record was broken with 8.3 inches on the 19th. Snow was recorded on all but two days during the month and measurable snow fell on 27 days including 23 days in a row from the 9th through the 31st.

# New Year's Day

The highest temperature ever recorded on New Year's Day was 63 degrees in 1985. The lowest the mercury has ever dropped to is zero in 1918 and 1970. Normally, the high temperature averages 34 degrees and the low about 20.

There is almost a 90 percent chance of precipitation of a trace or more, though not necessarily snow. The most precipitation ever on New Year's Day fell in 1932 when 1.40 inches was recorded. The most snow fell in 1964 totaling 8.1 inches between 2 p.m. and 8 p.m. Reduced visibilities and blowing snow were not a problem however as wind speeds were relatively low.

A severe winter storm began on New Year's Day in 1945 and before it was over on the 2nd, 15.0 inches of snow had fallen. The snow combined with winds of gale force resulted in another crippling of both city and inter city traffic and transportation by buses and street cars. Railway schedules were not abandoned but all passenger trains were several hours late. The storm was general throughout Western New York and many highways were impassable. Air travel was cancelled. Schools in the city and county closed.

**Period of record:** 101 years 1890-1990

**Temperature data:** New Year's Day

**Highest:**      63 degrees in 1985
**Lowest:**       0 degrees in 1918 & 1970

**Lowest maximum:**     11 degrees in 1918
**Highest maximum:**    37 degrees in 1950

**Average high temperature:**     34.2 degrees
**Average low temperature:**      20.5 degrees

**High temperature by 10 degree ranges:**

| Teens | 20s | 30s | 40s | 50s | 60s | |
|-------|-----|-----|-----|-----|-----|---|
| 9 | 28 | 37 | 16 | 10 | 1 | Number of occurrences |
| 9% | 28% | 36% | 16% | 10% | 1% | |

**Precipitation data:**

| | |
|---|---|
| Number of times with measurable precipitation | 66 or 66% |
| Number of times with a trace or more precipitation | 88 or 88% |
| Number of times with no precipitation | 13 or 12% |

**Snow:**   Number of times with a trace or more     71 occurrences
Number of times with over a trace      47 occurrences
Number of times with 1.0 inch or more      16 occurrences
Number of times with 5.0 inches or more     1 occurrence

**Maximum precipitation:**   1.40 inches in 1932

**Maximum snowfall:**        8.1 inches in 1964

| Date | Hi | Lo | Precip. | Remarks |
|------|----|----|---------|---------|
| 1983 | 39 | 30 | 0.1/0.1 | Cloudy, late morning snow flurries |
| 1984 | 30 | 22 | Tr/Tr | Cloudy, late night flurries |
| 1985 | 63 | 32 | 0.66/Tr | Cloudy, morning rain and freezing rain |
| 1986 | 29 | 20 | 0.03/0.3 | Cloudy, windy with light snow |
| 1987 | 36 | 27 | Tr/Tr | Cloudy, afternoon flurries |
| 1988 | 35 | 17 | 0.02/0.2 | Cloudy, occasional flurries |
| 1989 | 38 | 19 | 0.00 | M. sunny, increasing clouds late in the day |
| 1990 | 32 | 24 | Tr/Tr | Cloudy, morning flurries |

# Growing Season Data

Consider the growing season as the freeze-free period determined by the number of days between the last killing freeze (temperature 32 degrees or below) in the spring, and the first killing freeze in the fall (temperature 32 degrees or below) based on records from 1873 to 1985.

1.  Average date last spring minimum
    32 degrees or below . . . . . . . . . . . . . . . . . . . . . . . April 27

2   Average date first fall minimum
    32 degrees or below . . . . . . . . . . . . . . . . . . . . . October 24

3.  Average length of the growing season
    (April 27- October 24) . . . . . . . . . . . . . . . . . . . . . 180 days

4.  Shortest growing season of record . . . . . . . . . . . . . . 123 days
    (May 24, 1963 to September 24, 1963)

5.  Longest growing season of record . . . . . . . . . . . . . . 225 days
    (April 15, 1902 - November 26, 1902)

6.  Earliest date last spring minimum
    32 or below . . . . . . . . . . . . . . . . . . . . . . . March 30, 1878

7.  Latest date last spring minimum
    32 or below . . . . . . . . . . . . . . . . . . . May 24, 1925 & 1963

8.  Earliest date first fall minimum
    32 or below . . . . . . . . . . . . . . . . . . . September 23, 1947

9.  Latest date first fall minimum
    32 or below . . . . . . . . . . . . . . . . . . . . November 26, 1902

# Highest & Lowest
# Temperature by Month

|  | Highest Date/Year | Lowest Date/Year |
|---|---|---|
| January | 72 25th / 1950 | − 16 117th / 1982 |
| February | 70 21st / 1997* | − 21 9th / 1934 |
| March | 81 26th / 1945 | − 7 8 / 1984 |
| April | 88 23rd / 1985 28th / 1986 | 5 1st / 1923 |
| May | 94 22nd / 1911 | 25 4th / 1926 |
| June | 97 29th / 1933 | 35 1st / 1945 |
| July | 97 6th / 1988 | 43 11th / 1945 |
| August | 99 27th / 1948 | 38 30th / 1965 29th / 1982 |
| September | 98 3rd / 1953 | 32 23rd / 1947 28th / 1957 24th / 1963 |
| October | 92 2nd / 1927 | 20 29th / 1965 |
| November | 80 3rd / 1961 | 2 30th / 1875 |
| December | 74 3rd / 1982 | − 10 25th / 1980 |
| Annual | 99 August 27, 1948 | − 21 February 9, 1934 |

* Friday, Feb. 21, 1997 — 70 degrees sets record as warmest February day ever. Today's old record temperature of 62, was set in 1953. That was passed at 10 am, and by 12:15 p.m. the day had surpassed the February record of 68 set Feb. 11, 1932.

# Average Monthly Temperature Extremes Since 1871

|  | Warmest | | Coldest | |
|---|---|---|---|---|
| January | 37.2 | 1932 | 13.8 | 1977 |
| February | 33.8 | 1984 | 11.6 | 1934 |
| March | 44.5 | 1946 | 20.4 | 1885 |
| April | 51.3 | 1921 | 34.6 | 1874 |
| May | 63.4 | 1944 | 47.4 | 1917 |
| June | 72.5 | 1967 | 59.0 | 1926 |
| July | 76.2 | 1921 | 65.2 | 1884 |
| August | 75.2 | 1947 | 64.3 | 1963 |
| September | 71.2 | 1881 | 56.0 | 1918 |
| October | 60.5 | 1900 | 43.0 | 1925 |
| November | 47.9 | 1931 | 31.0 | 1873 |
| December | 37.6 | 1923 | 17.4 | 1989 |

**Warmest month:**   76.2 degrees — July 1921
**Coldest month:**   11.6 degrees — February 1934

*May of 1997 Coldest May in 30 years, May of 1997, had 28 consecutive days that were colder than normal. Longest stretch that spring didn't produce an 80 degree day. That didn't happen until June 16, 1997.*

# Ten Warmest Years

| | | |
|---|---|---|
| 1. | 50.6 | 1921 |
| 2. | 50.4 | 1949 |
| 3. | 50.4 | 1953 |
| 4. | 50.0 | 1931 |
| 5. | 49.9 | 1987 |
| 6. | 49.8 | 1898 |
| 7. | 49.5 | 1946 |
| 8. | 49.4 | 1955 |
| 9. | 49.4 | 1973 |
| 10. | 49.2 | 1952 |

# Ten Coldest Years

| | | |
|---|---|---|
| 1. | 43.0 | 1876 |
| 2. | 43.5 | 1917 |
| 3. | 44.1 | 1885 |
| 4. | 44.1 | 1926 |
| 5. | 44.7 | 1888 |
| 6. | 44.7 | 1904 |
| 7. | 45.0 | 1883 |
| 8. | 45.0 | 1924 |
| 9. | 45.4 | 1907 |
| 10. | 45.4 | 1943 |

# Greatest Number of Consecutive Days . . .

## With Maximum of 85 Degrees or Higher

**Number of Days**

| 12 | June 24 - July 5, 1949 |
|---|---|
| 9 | August 8 - 16, 1944 |
| | August 27 - September 4, 1953 |
| | July 29 - August 6, 1955 |
| | June 24 - July 2, 1963 |
| | July 20 - 28, 1964 |
| 8 | July 3 - 10, 1897 |
| | August 29 - September 5, 1973 |
| | July 13 - 20, 1983 |
| 7 | June 25 - July 1, 1946 |
| | July 22 - 28, 1963 |
| | July 17 - 23, 1972 |
| | July 19 - 25, 1987 |
| | July 4 - 10, 1988 |
| | August 8 - 14, 1988 |

## With Maximum of 90 Degrees or Higher:

**Number of Days**

| | |
|---|---|
| 7 | July 4 - 10, 1988 |
| 5 | August 10 - 14, 1947 |
| | June 27 - July 1, 1963 |
| 4 | August 1 - 4, 1944 |
| | September 1- 4, 1953 |
| | August 2 - 5, 1988 |
| | August 11 - 14, 1988 |
| 3 | August 9 -11, 1944 |
| | August 5 - 8, 1947 |
| | July 1 - 3, 1949 |
| | August 29 - 31, 1951 |
| | July 29 - 31, 1955 |
| | July 1 - 3, 1966 |
| | August 14 - 16, 1987 |

## With Maximum of 95 Degrees or Higher:

**Number of Days**

| | |
|---|---|
| 2 | August 1 - 2, 1944 |
| | July 5 - 6, 1988 |

## With Minimum of 65 Degrees or Higher:

**Number of Days**

| | |
|---|---|
| 26 | July 22 - August 16, 1939 |
| 25 | June 26 - July 20, 1921 |
| 19 | July 24 - August 11, 1938 |
| 18 | July 14 - July 31, 1898 |
| 17 | July 15 - 31, 1916 |
| 15 | July 22 - August 5, 1941 |
| 14 | August 1 - 14, 1984 |
| 13 | June 22 - July 4, 1894 |
| | August 5 - 17, 1920 |
| 12 | August 27 - September 7, 1981 |
| | June 25 - July 6, 1901 |
| | July 1 - 12, 1911 |
| | July 5 - 16, 1937 |
| | July 19 - 30, 1940 |

| 11 | August 24 - September 3, 1900 |
|    | July 14 - 24, 1901 |
|    | July 29 - August 8, 1911 |
|    | July 18 - 28, 1964 |
|    | August 26 - September 5, 1973 |
| 10 | August 2 - 11, 1906 |
|    | July 20 - 29, 1918 |
|    | August 1 - 10, 1928 |
|    | July 3 - 12, 1935 |
|    | August 3 - 12, 1937 |
|    | June 12 - 21, 1949 |
|    | August 26 - September 4, 1953 |
|    | August 24 - September 2, 1959 |
|    | June 7 - 16, 1967 |

# With Minimum of 70 Degrees or Higher:

**Number of Days**

| 9 | July 3 - 11, 1912 |
|   | July 22 - 30, 1940 |
| 8 | August 4 - 11, 1896 |
|   | July 3 - 10, 1921 |
|   | July 18 - 25, 1935 |
| 7 | July 19 - 25, 1916 |
|   | July 21 - 27, 1918 |
|   | July 8 - 14, 1936 |
|   | July 19 - 25, 1987 |
| 6 | July 1 - 6, 1887 |
|   | August 6 - 11, 1900 |
|   | June 29 - July 4, 1901 |
|   | August 1 - 6, 1911 |
|   | July 23 - 28, 1921 |
|   | July 23 - 28, 1941 |
|   | July 8 - 13, 1987 |
| 5 | August 17 - 21, 1884 |
|   | August 31 - September 4, 1898 |
|   | July 14 - 18, 1901 |
|   | July 2 - 6, 1901 |
|   | August 18 - 22, 1916 |
|   | September 10 - 14, 1931 |
|   | July 28 - August 1, 1933 |
|   | August 30 - September 3, 1937 |
|   | July 28 - August 1, 1970 |
|   | July 16 - 20, 1977 |

# With Minimum of 75 Degrees or Higher:

**Number of Days**

| | |
|---|---|
| 3 | September 1- 3, 1898 |
| 2 | August 5 - 6, 1876 |
| | July 17 - 18, 1876 |
| | July 9 - 10, 1897 |
| | August 10 - 11, 1900 |
| | June 3 - 4, 1919 |
| | July 6 - 7, 1921 |
| | July 12 - 13, 1936 |

# With Minimum of 20 Degrees or Less:

**Number of Days**

| | |
|---|---|
| 44 | January 26 - March 10, 1978 |
| 32 | January 8 - February 8, 1918 |
| 30 | January 17 - February 15, 1948 |
| 29 | January 16 - February 13, 1936 |
| | December 26, 1976 - January 23, 1977 |
| 28 | January 15 - February 11, 1985 |
| 27 | January 18 - February 13, 1961 |
| 25 | January 29 - February 27, 1875 |
| 23 | February 5 - 27, 1885 |
| 22 | January 9 - 30, 1888 |
| | January 27 - February 17, 1895 |
| | February 5 - 26, 1914 |
| 21 | January 31 - February 20, 1979 |
| | January 7 - 27, 1982 |
| 20 | December 19, 1878 - January 7, 1879 |
| | December 25, 1886 - January 13, 1887 |
| | January 3 - 22, 1893 |
| | January 27 - February 15, 1899 |
| | January 15 - February 3, 1940 |
| | December 30, 1980 - January 18, 1981 |

# With Minimum of 10 Degrees or Less:

**Number of Days**

| | |
|---|---|
| 17 | February 3 - 19, 1979 |
| 16 | February 4 - 19, 1875 |
| | January 19 - February 3, 1961 |
| 14 | January 4 - 17, 1912 |
| 12 | January 28 - February 8, 1905 |
| | January 26 - February 6, 1918 |
| | February 8 - 19, 1958 |
| 11 | January 10 - 20, 1893 |
| | January 22 - February 1, 1948 |
| 10 | February 16 - 25, 1885 |
| | January 20 - 29, 1988 |
| | January 23 - February 1, 1935 |
| | February 14 - 23, 1978 |
| 9 | January 6 -14, 1886 |
| | February 2 - 10, 1895 |
| | February 8 - 16, 1914 |
| | December 28, 1917 - January 5, 1918 |
| | January 26 - February 3, 1971 |
| 8 | March 16 - 23, 1885 |
| | February 18 - 25, 1914 |
| | March 6 - 13, 1960 |
| | February 20 - 27, 1963 |
| | March 2 - 9, 1978 |
| | January 30 - February 6, 1980 |
| | December 17 - 24, 1989 |
| 7 | February 1 - 7, 1881 |
| | February 28 - March 5, 1884 |
| | February 8 - 14, 1899 |
| | January 14 - 20, 1920 |
| | February 25 - March 2, 1920 |
| | January 28 - February 3, 1934 |
| | January 22 - 28, 1936 |
| | January 5 - 11, 1942 |
| | January 24 - 30, 1966 |
| | January 7 - 13, 1968 |
| | January 18 - 24, 1970 |
| | March 7 - 13, 1984 |

## With Minimum of Zero Degrees or Less:

**Number of Days**

| | |
|---|---|
| 6 | February 9 - 14, 1979 |
| 5 | February 6 - 10, 1875 |
| | February 12 - 16, 1875 |
| | February 2 - 6, 1881 |
| | February 10 - 14, 1885 |
| | February 5 - 9, 1895 |
| | February 9 - 13, 1899 |
| | February 9 - 13, 1917 |
| | December 28, 1917 - January 1, 1918 |
| 4 | December 29, 1880 - January 1, 1881 |
| | February 13 -16, 1905 |
| | January 5 - 8, 1912 |
| | February 7 - 10, 1934 |

## With Minimum of – 5 Degrees or Less:

**Number of Days**

| | |
|---|---|
| 4 | February 5 - 8, 1885 |
| 3 | February 10 - 12, 1885 |
| | February 14 - 16, 1905 |
| | February 9 - 11, 1912 |
| | February 11 - 13, 1914 |
| | February 11 - 13, 1917 |
| | February 8 - 10, 1934 |
| | January 13 - 15, 1957 |

## With a Minimum of –10 Degrees or Less

**Number of Days**

| | |
|---|---|
| 2 | February 8 - 9, 1934 |
| | February 11 - 12, 1979 |
| | January 16 - 17, 1982 |

# Greatest Number of Days in One Year . . .

## With Maximum of 95 Degrees or Higher:

6 in 1988 (1 in June, 4 in July, 1 in August)
3 in 1944 (1 in June, 2 in August)
1 in 1897, 1900, 1911, 1914, 1933, 1936, 1948,
1953, 1957, 1959)

## With Maximum of 90 Degrees or Higher:

20 in 1955
18 in 1988
15 in 1944
13 in 1947 and 1959
12 in 1953
11 in 1952

## With Maximum of 32 Degrees or Lower:

76 in 1917 and 1960
75 in 1903 and 1978
72 in 1926
71 in 1872 and 1904
70 in 1875 and 1893

# Greatest Number of Days in One Month . . .

## With Maximum of 95 Degrees or Higher:

4 in July, 1988
2 in August, 1944

## With Maximum of 90 Degrees or Higher:

13 in July 1955
9 in August 1988 and August 1944
8 in July 1988
7 in August 1959
6 in July 1952

## With Maximum of 32 Degrees or Lower:

29 in January 1945
28 in January 1881 and February 1978**
27 in January 1897, February 1901, January 1903,
and January 1918

**February 1978 only entire month of maximum 32
degrees or less.

## With Maximum of 70 Degrees or Higher:

25 in 1900
24 in 1898
22 in 1901, 1926, 1921
21 in 1937
18 in 1931
17 in 1887, 1911, 1935
16 in 1876, 1938, 1940, 1983, 1987
15 in 1906, 1941, 1955, 1973

## With Minimum of 75 Degrees or Higher:

5 in 1900
4 in 1988
3 in 1897, 1898, 1901, 1911, 1918

## With Minimum of 32 Degrees of Lower:

161 in 1962
155 in 1926
153 in 1947
152 in 1943
150 in 1972

## With Minimum of Zero Degrees or Lower:

17 in 1875
16 in 1885
13 in 1917
12 in 1904, 1934, 1979

# Greatest Number of Days in One Month . . .

## With Minimum of 70 Degrees or Higher:

19 in July 1921
14 in July 1901
13 in July 1887, July 1898, July 1916, July 1935
12 in August 1900

## With Minimum of 75 Degrees or Higher:

4 in August 1900, August 1988
3 in July 1897, July 1901

## With Minimum of Zero Degrees of Lower:

12 in February 1875
11 in February 1934
10 in February 1885
9 in February 1979

# Greatest Temperature Change in a 24 Hour Day

**47 degrees on two occasions:**

| | |
|---|---|
| November 12, 1911 | 69 degrees at 6 a.m. falling to 22 degrees at midnight |
| December 8, 1927 | 59 degrees at 2 a.m. falling to 12 degrees at midnight |

# Greatest Temperature Rise in a 24 Hour Day

**46 degrees**

May 5, 1950 — 44 degrees at 5 a.m. rising to 90 degrees at 3:30 p.m.

# Least Temperature Change in a 24 Hour Day

**1 degree**

November 29, 1928 — Maximum 38 degrees  Minimum 37 degrees
Last of several

# 20 Rainiest 24 Hour Periods
## Since 1871

| | | |
|---|---|---|
| 1. | 5.01 inches | June 22, 1987 |
| 2. | 4.94 inches | September 13 - 14, 1979 |
| 3. | 4.28 inches | August 28 - 29, 1893 |
| 4. | 3.88 inches | August 7, 1963 |
| 5. | 3.65 inches | August 17, 1944 |
| 6. | 3.63 inches | September 27 - 28, 1967 |
| 7. | 3.57 inches | August 29 - 30, 1975 |
| 8. | 3.56 inches | July 19 - 20,1896 |
| 9. | 3.52 inches | May 19 - 20, 1986 |
| 10. | 3.49 inches | October 1-2, 1945 |
| 11. | 3.38 inches | July 29, 1963 |
| 12. | 3.28 inches | June 21 - 22, 1885 |
| 13. | 3.23 inches | August 27 - 28, 1871 |
| 14. | 3.11 inches | October 5 - 6, 1955 |
| 15. | 3.10 inches | October 2 - 3, 1881 |
| 16. | 3.10 inches | July 24 - 25, 1910 |
| 17. | 3.04 inches | June 25 - 26, 1968 |
| 18. | 3.01 inches | June 9, 1989 |
| 19. | 2.93 inches | September 17 - 18, 1976 |
| 20. | 2.91 inches | July 19 - 20, 1911 |

# Precipitation — Greatest in 24 Hours
## (Since 1871)

| | | |
|---|---|---|
| January | 2.57 inches | January 10 - 11, 1982 |
| February | 2.31 inches | February 16 - 17, 1954 |
| March | 2.62 inches | March 17, 1936 |
| April | 1.94 inches | April 3 - 4, 1903 |
| May | 3.52 inches | May 19 - 20, 1986 |
| June | 5.01 inches | June 22, 1987 |
| July | 3.56 inches | July 19 - 20, 1896 |
| August | 4.28 inches | August 28 - 29, 1893 |
| September | 4.94 inches | September 13 - 14, 1979 |
| October | 3.49 inches | October 1 - 2, 1945 |
| November | 2.82 inches | November 16 - 17, 1920 |
| December | 2.53 inches | December 22 - 23, 1878 |
| Annual | 5.01 inches | June 22, 1987 |

# Greatest Amount of Snow in 24 Hours
## (Since 1890)

| | | |
|---|---|---|
| 1. | 37.9 inches | December 9-10, 1995 |
| 2. | 25.3 inches | January 10 - 11, 1982 |
| 3. | 24.3 inches | December 15 - 16, 1945 |
| 4. | 21.6 inches | January 10 - 11, 1997 |
| 5. | 20.1 inches | November 30 - December 1, 1979 |
| 6. | 19.9 inches | November 28 - 29, 1955 |
| 7. | 19.4 inches | February 27 - 28, 1984 |
| 8. | 19.0 inches | November 30, 1976 |
| 9. | 19.0 inches | March 17, 1936 |

| 10. | 18.2 inches | January 22 - 23, 1966 |
| 11. | 17.8 inches | December 30, 1961 |
| 12. | 17.4 inches | November 15 - 16, 1949 |
| 13. | 17.4 inches | January 21 - 22, 1902 |
| 14. | 16.9 inches | January 19 - 20, 1985 |
| 15. | 16.1 inches | February 11 - 12, 1910 |
| 16. | 16.0 inches | December 26 - 27, 1956 |
| 17. | 15.8 inches | March 29 - 30, 1954 |
| 18. | 15.0 inches | December 16, 1900 |
| 19. | 15.0 inches | December 16, 1926 |
| 20. | 14.8 inches | November 16 - 17, 1958 |
| 21. | 14.5 inches | February 16 - 17, 1958 |
| 22. | 14.0 inches | January 3, 1928 |
| 23. | 14.0 inches | December 8 - 9, 1977 |
| 24. | 14.0 inches | January 31 - February 1, 1979 |

# Greatest Depth of Snow on Ground

## (Since 1893)

| September | Trace | 23rd, 1950 |
| | | 20th, 1956 |
| October | 4.5 inches | 29th, 1895 |
| November | 21 inches | 30th, 1976 |
| December | 33 inches | 9th and 10th, 1995 |
| January | 38 inches | 29th, 30th, and 31st, 1977 |
| February | 43 inches | 5th and 6th, 1977 |
| March | 25 inches | 2nd, 1900 |
| April | 13 inches | 5th, 1975 |
| May | 4 inches | 7th, 1989 |

Greatest depth on record: 43 inches — February 5th and 6th, 1977

# First Snowfall in Fall:

Average date of first trace of snow:  . . . . . . . .  October 24

Average date of first measurable snow:  . . . . .  November 8

Average date of first 1 inch or more snow:  . . .  November 17

Earliest snowfall of trace or more:  . . . . . . . . .  September 20, 1956

Earliest measurable snowfall:  . . . . . . . . . . . .  October 9, 1925

Earliest snowfall of 1 inch or more:  . . . . . . . .  October 10, 1906

Latest first snowfall of trace or more:  . . . . . . .  November 22, 1946
and 1985

Latest first measurable snowfall:  . . . . . . . . . .  December 3, 1899

Latest first snowfall of 1 inch or more:  . . . . . .  January 2, 1932

# Last Snowfall in Spring

Average date of last trace or more of snow:  . .  April 27

Average date of last measurable snow:  . . . . . .  April 19

Average date of last 1 inch or more snowfall:  .  April 3

Earliest date of last snow of trace or more:  . . .  April 1, 1941

Earliest date of last measurable snowfall:  . . . .  March 21, 1951

Earliest date of last 1 inch or more snowfall:  .  February 12, 1925

Latest date of snowfall of trace or more:  . . . .  June 10, 1980

Latest date of measurable snowfall:  . . . . . . . .  May 20, 1907

Latest date of 1 inch or more snowfall:  . . . . .  May 10, 1923
and 1945

# Average Number of Days with Snowfall of . . .

## (Since 1884/85)

|  | 0.1 or more | 1.0 or more | 3.0 or more | 6.0 or more | 10.0 or more |
|---|---|---|---|---|---|
| October | * | * | * | * | * |
| November | 5.4 | 2.5 | 0.9 | * | * |
| December | 13.2 | 5.2 | 1.9 | 0.6 | * |
| January | 16.1 | 6.6 | 2.0 | * | * |
| February | 13.9 | 5.4 | 2.2 | * | * |
| March | 9.9" | 3.4 | 0.8 | * | * |
| April | 3.3" | 1.0 | * | * | * |
| May | * | * |  |  |  |
| **Seasonal** | 62.3 | 24.1 | 7.3 | 2.0 | 0.6 |
| **Maximum** | 99 1976-77 | 52 1976-77 | 21 1976-77 | 6 1885-86 1976-77 | 4 1976-77 |
| **Minimum** | 21 1889-90 | 8 1889-90 | 0 1918-19 | 0 many | 0 many |

\* less than one

# The Snowiest Years

| 1. | 1976-77 | 199.4 inches |
|---|---|---|
| 2. | 1977-78 | 154.3 inches |
| 3. | 1995-96 | 141.1 inches |
| 4. | 1983-84 | 132.5 inches |
| 5. | 1909-10 | 126.4 inches |

# Consecutive Number of Days with Measurable Snowfall

| | |
|---|---|
| 28 | December 26, 1976 - January 22, 1977 |
| 24 | December 9, 1985 - January 1, 1986 |
| 19 | February 6, 1962 - February 24, 1962 |
| 18 | January 27, 1901 - February 13, 1901 |
| | January 7, 1970 - January 24, 1970 |
| 16 | January 4, 1903 - January 19, 1903 |
| | December 7, 1904 - December 22, 1904 |
| | December 29, 1968 - January 13, 1969 |
| 15 | January 15, 1940 - January 29, 1940 |
| 14 | December 11, 1969 - December 24, 1969 |
| | December 9, 1973 - December 22, 1973 |
| | January 24, 1977 - February 6, 1977 |
| 13 | January 7, 1918 - January 19, 1918 |
| | December 12, 1963 - December 24, 1963 |
| | February 14, 1973 - February 26, 1973 |
| 12 | January 23, 1898 - February 3, 1898 |
| | December 11, 1950 - December 22, 1950 |
| | January 21, 1955 - February 1, 1955 |
| | February 7, 1963 - February 18, 1963 |
| | December 19, 1966 - December 30, 1966 |
| | November 28, 1976 - December 9, 1976 |
| | January 26, 1987 - February 7, 1978 |
| | February 2, 1988 - February 13, 1988 |
| 11 | January 30, 1902 - February 9, 1902 |
| | December 4, 1903 - December 14, 1903 |
| | December 25, 1903 - January 4, 1904 |
| | February 3, 1916 - February 13, 1916 |
| | January 2, 1942 - January 12, 1942 |
| | February 18, 1972 - February 28, 1972 |
| | January 8, 1978 - January 18, 1978 |
| | December 9, 1980 - December 19, 1980 |
| | January 17, 1985 - January 27, 1985 |
| | February 7, 1986 - February 17, 1986 |
| | February 2, 1989 - February 12, 1989 |

# Other Snow Data

Most of our snow is of the 1-2" variety — about 24 times a season. We average only 2 storms a season with more than 6"

**(City Averages)**
Buffalo 92"
Rochester 88"
Syracuse 110"
South of Buffalo over 12 feet
East of Lake Ontario 10-17 feet
(See its not so bad after all.)

# Consecutive Number of Days with Measurable Precipitation
## (Rain, Snow, or Rain and Snow)

| | |
|---|---|
| 24 | December 9, 1985 - January 1, 1986 |
| 20 | December 16, 1903 - January 4, 1904 |
| 19 | December 7, 1904 - December 25, 1904 |
| | January 20, 1978 - February 7, 1978 |
| 18 | January 27, 1901 - February 13, 1901 |
| | January 2, 1903 - January 19, 1903 |
| | January 2, 1905 - January 19, 1905 |
| 17 | January 31, 1904 - February 16, 1904 |
| | January 6, 1977 - January 22, 1977 |
| 16 | January 31, 1905 - February 15, 1905 |
| | January 14, 1940 - January 29, 1940 |
| 15 | December 17, 1878 - December 31, 1878 |
| | January 16, 1941 - January 30, 1941 |
| | February 1, 1989 - February 15, 1989    (R&S) |
| 14 | January 6, 1918 - January 19, 1918 |
| | February 5, 1920 - February 18, 1920 |
| | February 2, 1924 - February 15, 1924 |
| | November 24, 1976 - December 7, 1976 |
| | January 24, 1977 - February 6, 1977 |
| | January 31, 1988 - February 13, 1988 |

| 13 | April 22, 1878 - May 4, 1878 ** | ** Maximum |
|---|---|---|
|  | May 30, 1889 - June 11, 1889 ** | Consecutive |
|  | December 21, 1956 - January 2, 1957 | Days of Rain |
|  | December 12, 1963 - December 24, 1963 |  |
|  | December 7, 1980 - December 19, 1980 |  |
|  | November 2, 1985 - November14, 1985 |  |
|  | February 7, 1986 - February 19, 1986 |  |

| 12 | January 14, 1907 - January 25, 1907 |
|---|---|
|  | January 28, 1908 - February 8, 1908 |
|  | December 11, 1916 - December 22, 1916 |
|  | December 11, 1950 - December 22, 1950 |
|  | January 21, 1955 - February 1, 1955 |
|  | February 7, 1963 - February 18, 1963 |
|  | March 29, 1974 - April 9, 1974 |
|  | December 30, 1978 - January 10, 1979 |
|  | March 9, 1981 - March 20, 1981 |

# Wind Gusts — Over 70 mph
## (Since July 1, 1943)

| 91 mph* | SW | January 14, 1950 |
|---|---|---|
| 82 mph | SW | February 16, 1967 |
| 81 mph | W | August 24, 1972 |
| 79 mph | S | June 7, 1980 |
| 74 mph | W | April 6, 1985 |
| 72 mph | W | March 10, 1986 |
|  | SW | April 30, 1984 |
| 71 mph | W | August 15, 1988 |
|  | SW | January 1, 1985 |
| 70 mph | SW | January 26, 1965 |
| 70 mph* | SW | February 14, 1946 |
| 70 mph* | SW | January 10, 1950 |

(*Fastest Mile)

# 22 Peak Gusts

## (Since December 10, 1960)

(All times EST)

| | | | |
|---|---|---|---|
| 82 mph | SW | February 16, 1967 | 0422 |
| 81 mph | W | August 24, 1972 | 1847 |
| 79 mph | S | June 7, 1980 | 2033 |
| 74 mph | W | April 6, 1985 | 0217 |
| 72 mph | W | March 10, 1986 | 1815 |
| | SW | April 30, 1984 | 1701 |
| 71 mph | W | August 15, 1988 | 0157 |
| | SW | January 1, 1985 | 1726 |
| 70 mph | SW | January 26, 1965 | 1922 |
| 69 mph | SW | January 28, 1977 | 1733 |
| | SW | December 15, 1971 | 2140 |
| 68 mph | W | November 10, 1988 | 1151 |
| | W | March 11, 1986 | 0403 |
| | SW | August 17, 1965 | 1458 |
| 67 mph | W | January 5, 1982 | 0005 |
| | SW | March 27, 1976 | 1454 |
| | SW | December 22, 1967 | 0056 |
| | SW | March 5, 1964 | 1508 |
| 66 mph | SW | December 2, 1985 | 1058 |
| | SW | December 28, 1982 | 2214 |
| | S | January 11, 1980 | 1114 |
| | S | January 26, 1978 | 0843 |
| | SW | January 27, 1974 | 0636 |
| | W | January 25, 1972 | 0850 |

# Record Peak Gusts for Each Month

## (All times EST)

| | | | | |
|---|---|---|---|---|
| January | 71 mph | SW | 1726 | January 1, 1985 |
| February | 82 mph | SW | 0422 | February 16, 1967 |
| March | 72 mph | W | 1815 | March 10, 1986 |
| April | 74 mph | W | 0217 | April 6, 1985 |
| May | 65 mph | SW | 0138 | May 17, 1974* |
| June | 79 mph | S | 2033 | June 7, 1980 |
| July | 59 mph | W | 1751 | July 31, 1977 |
| August | 81 mph | W | 1847 | August 24, 1972 |
| September | 62 mph | S | 1720 | September 29, 1987 |
| October | 63 mph | W | 1341 | October 31, 1965 |
| November | 68 mph | W | 1151 | November 10,1988 |
| December | 69 mph | SW | 2140 | December 15, 1971 |
| Year | 82 mph | SW | 0422 | February 16, 1967 |

*Last of several

# 20 Fastest Miles

## (Since July 1, 1943)

| | | |
|---|---|---|
| 91 mph | SW | January 14, 1950 |
| 70 mph | SW | January 10, 1950 |
| | SW | February 14, 1946 |
| 69 mph | SW | February 21, 1953 |
| 68 mph | W | March 7, 1959 |
| 67 mph | W | April 25,1957 |
| 66 mph | SW | March 24, 1951 |
| | SW | November 17, 1948 |
| | SW | March 16, 1948 |

| 65 mph | W | March 16, 1959 |
|---|---|---|
| | SW | March 6, 1959 |
| | W | January 22, 1959 |
| | SW | November 8, 1957 |
| | W | April 20, 1948 |
| 64 mph | SW | November 16, 1955 |
| 63 mph | SW | October 15, 1954 |
| | SW | May 6, 1950 |
| 62 mph | SW | February 16, 1967 |
| | SW | May 22, 1945 |
| 61 mph | SW | January 11, 1950 |

# Record Fastest Miles for Each Month
## (Since July 1, 1943)

| January | 91 mph | SW | January 14, 1950 |
|---|---|---|---|
| February | 70 mph | SW | February 14, 1946 |
| March | 68 mph | W | March 7, 1959 |
| April | 67 mph | W | April 25, 1957 |
| May | 63 mph | SW | May 6, 1950 |
| June | 56 mph | NNW | June 12, 1954 |
| July | 59 mph | NW | July 1, 1953 |
| August | 56 mph | SW | August 12, 1944 |
| September | 59 mph | SW | September 21, 1954 |
| October | 63 mph | SW | October 15, 1954 |
| November | 66 mph | SW | November 17, 1948 |
| December | 60 mph | S | December 25, 1945 |
| Year | 91 mph | SW | January 14, 1950 |

# 20 Windiest Days
## (Since July 1, 1943 – Average Wind Speed)

| | |
|---|---|
| 36.8 mph | February 21, 1953 |
| 36.4 mph | January 24, 1982 |
| 35.5 mph | January 22,1959 |
| 35.4 mph | January 6, 1949 |
| 35.0 mph | November 17, 1955 |
| 34.2 mph | March 23, 1955 |
| 34.1 mph | January 14, 1950 |
| 34.0 mph | December 22, 1951 |
| 33.7 mph | May 6, 1950 |
| 33.5 mph | January 31, 1966 |
| 32.9 mph | January 26, 1978 |
| 32.7 mph | April 6, 1985 |
| 32.7 mph | January 19,1949 |
| 32.4 mph | October 28, 1983 |
| 32.0 mph | February 2, 1985 |
| 32.0 mph | January 31, 1946 |
| 31.9 mph | June 29, 1957 |
| 31.9 mph | March 25, 1947 |
| 31.8 mph | January 16, 1950 |
| 31.6 mph | December 17, 1946 |

# Record Windy Days for Each Month
## (Since July 1, 1943 – Average Wind Speed)

| | | |
|---|---|---|
| January | 36.4 mph | January 24, 1982 |
| February | 36.8 mph | February 21, 1953 |
| March | 34.2 mph | March 23, 1955 |
| April | 32.7 mph | April 6, 1985 |
| May | 33.7 mph | May 6, 1950 |
| June | 31.9 mph | June 29, 1957 |
| July | 29.5 mph | July 1, 1977 |
| August | * | |
| September | 26.2 mph | September 27, 1951 |
| October | 32.4 mph | October 28, 1983 |
| November | 35.0 mph | November 17, 1955 |
| December | 34.0 mph | December 22, 1951 |

* less than 25.0 mph

# Weather IQ

1. A halo around the moon means?
   - a. sunny day tomorrow
   - b. rain and snow
   - c. windy

2. If an owl hoots at night be ready for?
   - a. snowstorm
   - b. rain
   - c. big changes

3. A rainbow in the morning means?
   - a. rain soon
   - b. good weather
   - c. colder

4. Red sky in the morning means?
   - a. rain
   - b. fair
   - c. warmer

5. Red sky at night means
   - a. fair
   - b. wind
   - c. rain

Answers 1: b, 2: c, 3: a, 4: a, 5: a

# Farewell . . .

And so I have run out of weather stories, and trivia for our fine area of the world. Some people will always criticize Buffalo for the "bad" weather we are supposed to have. And I must accept the fact that no amount of "hype," no amount of positive weather stories will ever change some peoples thoughts about Buffalo's weather.

Without any further denials, or statements that the critics don't know what they are talking about, I will simply say . . . Lets not spread the truth about our weather anymore. Lets just keep it our secret. And enjoy the four seasons, each beautiful and remarkable for certain specific reasons. Let's keep this area a secret, so we can enjoy it all ourselves.

# Bolts From the Blue:
# The Mystery of Lightning

Imagine being Roy C. Sullivan, a Virginia man who has the dubious distinction of being the human being struck by lightning the most times. According to the *Guinness Book of World Records,* Sullivan was struck by lightning seven times in his life.

But why does lightning occur?

The truth is, experts don't know too much more about the cause of lightning than Ben Franklin did when he experimented with a kite way back in 1752.

While lightning remains a mysterious phenomenon the *Scientific American* serves up some -- shall we say "jolting" meteorological tidbits:

- A single lightning bolt carries a powerful electric current of up to 300,000 amperes. A single strike of lightning contains 100 million volts of electricity and can easily destroy any object caught in its path. Compare the awesome power of a lightning bolt with the wiring in a typical house which carries only a few tens of amperes.

- Lightning is responsible for about half of all power failures in regions which are prone to thunderstorms. Such power failures cost utility companies as much as $1 billion a year in damaged equipment and lost revenue.

- Each year about 20 million individual flashes of lightning hit the ground. The Empire State Building gets hit by lightning an average of 23 times a year.

- Lightning kills several hundred people each year.

- The National Lightning Network consists of more than 100 stations across the country. These stations analyze lightning by sensing the precise timing and direction of the bursts of electromagnetic energy emitted by these changes.

- You may have heard about some folks who have sighted strange globes of moving energy. Scientists report that these "ball lightning" sightings are actually miniature comet-like bodies which are constantly pelting the earth's atmosphere.

- Researchers have been finding some exciting new ways to control lightning with lasers.

# More About Tornadoes

Who can forget those vivid celluloid moments when a twister delivers wide-eyed Dorothy to the magical land of Oz.

While tornadoes have been spotted throughout the world, they are more common in North America than in any other region on Earth. New York State averages about five tornadoes annually, with two twisters reported in our region in a typical year. Chautauqua County has the dubious distinction of having the most tornadoes, with 18 reported over a 41-year period. Other counties across the state average one tornado every five to ten years.

Most tornadoes in New York occur in May, June or July when temperatures between colliding air masses are generally not as extreme. Tornadoes descend from thunderstorms under a variety of conditions. Most dangerous storms occur when high speed jet streams flow atop clashing warm and cold air masses. Warm temperatures, high winds and high humidity are often early warning signs.

How do forecasters predict tornadoes? Twice each day weather wizards launch balloons to measure pressure, winds, temperature and moisture in the atmosphere from the surface of the Earth. The data is sorted and analyzed by computers at the National Meteorological Center in Washington, D.C. Information gathered from airplanes and satellites are also scrutinized. The computer forecasts are then relayed to local weather offices across the country.

In the last 50 years, more than 23,000 tornadoes have struck the U.S., claiming more than 7,000 lives. The Insurance Information Institute encourages people to take tornado warnings seriously.

Experts underscore the importance of making sure that everyone in a household knows in advance where to go and what to do in case of a tornado warning. One important tip: stay calm. Don't attempt to flee from the path of a tornado in a vehicle. Cars or trucks are no match for a tornado which can have wind speeds exceeding 200 miles an hour.

If you're home or at work, stay inside and away from windows and exterior walls until the tornado is over. The safest place in a home is in the basement. If there's no basement, take shelter in a closet, bathroom or under a heavy piece of furniture on the lowest level of the home."

After a tornado has struck, be alert for potential hazards such as downed power lines, splintered wood and shattered glass.

# Eastern Standard Time

| Day | JAN. Rise A.M. | JAN. Set P.M. | FEB. Rise A.M. | FEB. Set P.M. | MAR. Rise A.M. | MAR. Set P.M. | APR. Rise A.M. | APR. Set P.M. | MAY Rise A.M. | MAY Set P.M. | JUNE Rise A.M. | JUNE Set P.M. |
|---|---|---|---|---|---|---|---|---|---|---|---|---|
| 1 | 7:46 | 4:51 | 7:30 | 5:27 | 6:51 | 6:04 | 5:58 | 6:41 | 5:09 | 7:15 | 4:39 | 7:47 |
| 2 | 7:46 | 4:52 | 7:29 | 5:29 | 6:50 | 6:05 | 5:56 | 6:42 | 5:08 | 7:17 | 4:38 | 7:48 |
| 3 | 7:46 | 4:53 | 7:28 | 5:30 | 6:48 | 6:06 | 5:54 | 6:43 | 5:07 | 7:18 | 4:38 | 7:48 |
| 4 | 7:46 | 4:54 | 7:27 | 5:31 | 6:46 | 6:08 | 5:52 | 6:44 | 5:05 | 7:19 | 4:37 | 7:49 |
| 5 | 7:46 | 4:55 | 7:26 | 5:33 | 6:45 | 6:09 | 5:51 | 6:45 | 5:04 | 7:20 | 4:37 | 7:50 |
| 6 | 7:46 | 4:56 | 7:25 | 5:34 | 6:43 | 6:10 | 5:49 | 6:47 | 5:03 | 7:21 | 4:37 | 7:51 |
| 7 | 7:46 | 4:57 | 7:23 | 5:35 | 6:41 | 6:11 | 5:47 | 6:48 | 5:01 | 7:22 | 4:36 | 7:51 |
| 8 | 7:46 | 4:58 | 7:22 | 5:37 | 6:40 | 6:13 | 5:45 | 6:49 | 5:00 | 7:23 | 4:36 | 7:52 |
| 9 | 7:46 | 4:59 | 7:21 | 5:38 | 6:38 | 6:14 | 5:44 | 6:50 | 4:59 | 7:24 | 4:36 | 7:52 |
| 10 | 7:45 | 5:00 | 7:20 | 5:39 | 6:36 | 6:15 | 5:42 | 6:51 | 4:58 | 7:25 | 4:36 | 7:53 |
| 11 | 7:45 | 5:01 | 7:18 | 5:41 | 6:35 | 6:16 | 5:40 | 6:52 | 4:57 | 7:27 | 4:36 | 7:54 |
| 12 | 7:45 | 5:02 | 7:17 | 5:42 | 6:33 | 6:17 | 5:39 | 6:54 | 4:55 | 7:28 | 4:35 | 7:54 |
| 13 | 7:44 | 5:03 | 7:16 | 5:43 | 6:31 | 6:19 | 5:37 | 6:55 | 4:54 | 7:29 | 4:35 | 7:55 |
| 14 | 7:44 | 5:05 | 7:14 | 5:45 | 6:29 | 6:20 | 5:35 | 6:56 | 4:53 | 7:30 | 4:35 | 7:55 |
| 15 | 7:43 | 5:06 | 7:13 | 5:46 | 6:28 | 6:21 | 5:34 | 6:57 | 4:52 | 7:31 | 4:35 | 7:55 |
| 16 | 7:43 | 5:07 | 7:11 | 5:47 | 6:26 | 6:22 | 5:32 | 6:58 | 4:51 | 7:32 | 4:35 | 7:56 |
| 17 | 7:42 | 5:08 | 7:10 | 5:49 | 6:24 | 6:23 | 5:30 | 6:59 | 4:50 | 7:33 | 4:35 | 7:56 |
| 18 | 7:42 | 5:09 | 7:09 | 5:50 | 6:22 | 6:25 | 5:29 | 7:00 | 4:49 | 7:34 | 4:35 | 7:56 |
| 19 | 7:41 | 5:11 | 7:07 | 5:51 | 6:21 | 6:26 | 5:27 | 7:02 | 4:48 | 7:35 | 4:36 | 7:57 |
| 20 | 7:41 | 5:12 | 7:06 | 5:53 | 6:19 | 6:27 | 5:26 | 7:03 | 4:47 | 7:36 | 4:36 | 7:57 |
| 21 | 7:40 | 5:13 | 7:04 | 5:54 | 6:17 | 6:28 | 5:24 | 7:04 | 4:46 | 7:37 | 4:36 | 7:57 |
| 22 | 7:39 | 5:14 | 7:03 | 5:55 | 6:15 | 6:29 | 5:23 | 7:05 | 4:46 | 7:38 | 4:36 | 7:57 |
| 23 | 7:38 | 5:16 | 7:01 | 5:56 | 6:13 | 6:30 | 5:21 | 7:06 | 4:45 | 7:39 | 4:36 | 7:58 |
| 24 | 7:38 | 5:17 | 6:59 | 5:58 | 6:12 | 6:32 | 5:19 | 7:07 | 4:44 | 7:40 | 4:37 | 7:58 |
| 25 | 7:37 | 5:18 | 6:58 | 5:59 | 6:10 | 6:33 | 5:18 | 7:09 | 4:43 | 7:41 | 4:37 | 7:58 |
| 26 | 7:36 | 5:20 | 6:56 | 6:00 | 6:08 | 6:34 | 5:17 | 7:10 | 4:42 | 7:42 | 4:37 | 7:58 |
| 27 | 7:35 | 5:21 | 6:55 | 6:01 | 6:06 | 6:35 | 5:15 | 7:11 | 4:42 | 7:43 | 4:38 | 7:58 |
| 28 | 7:34 | 5:22 | 6:53 | 6:03 | 6:05 | 6:36 | 5:14 | 7:12 | 4:41 | 7:44 | 4:38 | 7:58 |
| 29 | 7:33 | 5:23 | 6:52 | 6:04 | 6:03 | 6:37 | 5:12 | 7:13 | 4:40 | 7:44 | 4:39 | 7:58 |
| 30 | 7:32 | 5:25 |  |  | 6:01 | 6:39 | 5:11 | 7:14 | 4:40 | 7:45 | 4:39 | 7:58 |
| 31 | 7:31 | 5:26 |  |  | 5:59 | 6:40 |  |  | 4:39 | 7:46 |  |  |

Daylight Saving Time: Add an hour.

*U.S. Naval Observeratory*

# Eastern Standard Time

| Day | JULY Rise A.M. | JULY Set P.M. | AUG. Rise A.M. | AUG. Set P.M. | SEPT. Rise A.M. | SEPT. Set P.M. | OCT. Rise A.M. | OCT. Set P.M. | NOV. Rise A.M. | NOV. Set P.M. | DEC. Rise A.M. | DEC. Set P.M. |
|---|---|---|---|---|---|---|---|---|---|---|---|---|
| 1 | 4:40 | 7:58 | 5:05 | 7:36 | 5:39 | 6:50 | 6:12 | 5:57 | 6:49 | 5:08 | 7:26 | 4:42 |
| 2 | 4:40 | 7:57 | 5:07 | 7:35 | 5:40 | 6:48 | 6:13 | 5:55 | 6:50 | 5:06 | 7:27 | 4:41 |
| 3 | 4:41 | 7:57 | 5:08 | 7:34 | 5:41 | 6:47 | 6:14 | 5:53 | 6:52 | 5:05 | 7:28 | 4:41 |
| 4 | 4:41 | 7:57 | 5:09 | 7:33 | 5:42 | 6:45 | 6:15 | 5:51 | 6:53 | 5:04 | 7:29 | 4:41 |
| 5 | 4:42 | 7:57 | 5:10 | 7:31 | 5:43 | 6:43 | 6:16 | 5:50 | 6:54 | 5:03 | 7:30 | 4:41 |
| 6 | 4:42 | 7:56 | 5:11 | 7:30 | 5:44 | 6:41 | 6:17 | 5:48 | 6:55 | 5:01 | 7:31 | 4:41 |
| 7 | 4:43 | 7:56 | 5:12 | 7:29 | 5:45 | 6:40 | 6:19 | 5:46 | 6:57 | 5:00 | 7:32 | 4:40 |
| 8 | 4:44 | 7:56 | 5:13 | 7:27 | 5:47 | 6:38 | 6:20 | 5:45 | 6:58 | 4:59 | 7:33 | 4:40 |
| 9 | 4:44 | 7:55 | 5:14 | 7:26 | 5:48 | 6:36 | 6:21 | 5:43 | 6:59 | 4:58 | 7:34 | 4:40 |
| 10 | 4:45 | 7:55 | 5:15 | 7:25 | 5:49 | 6:34 | 6:22 | 5:41 | 7:00 | 4:57 | 7:35 | 4:40 |
| 11 | 4:46 | 7:54 | 5:16 | 7:23 | 5:50 | 6:33 | 6:23 | 5:39 | 7:02 | 4:56 | 7:36 | 4:40 |
| 12 | 4:47 | 7:54 | 5:17 | 7:22 | 5:51 | 6:31 | 6:24 | 5:38 | 7:03 | 4:55 | 7:37 | 4:41 |
| 13 | 4:48 | 7:53 | 5:18 | 7:20 | 5:52 | 6:29 | 6:26 | 5:36 | 7:04 | 4:54 | 7:37 | 4:41 |
| 14 | 4:48 | 7:53 | 5:19 | 7:19 | 5:53 | 6:27 | 6:27 | 5:34 | 7:06 | 4:53 | 7:38 | 4:41 |
| 15 | 4:49 | 7:52 | 5:20 | 7:18 | 5:54 | 6:25 | 6:28 | 5:33 | 7:07 | 4:52 | 7:39 | 4:41 |
| 16 | 4:50 | 7:51 | 5:22 | 7:16 | 5:55 | 6:24 | 6:29 | 5:31 | 7:08 | 4:51 | 7:40 | 4:41 |
| 17 | 4:51 | 7:51 | 5:23 | 7:15 | 5:56 | 6:22 | 6:30 | 5:30 | 7:09 | 4:50 | 7:40 | 4:42 |
| 18 | 4:52 | 7:50 | 5:24 | 7:13 | 5:57 | 6:20 | 6:32 | 5:28 | 7:11 | 4:49 | 7:41 | 4:42 |
| 19 | 4:53 | 7:49 | 5:25 | 7:11 | 5:59 | 6:18 | 6:33 | 5:26 | 7:12 | 4:48 | 7:42 | 4:42 |
| 20 | 4:54 | 7:48 | 5:26 | 7:10 | 6:00 | 6:16 | 6:34 | 5:25 | 7:13 | 4:48 | 7:42 | 4:43 |
| 21 | 4:55 | 7:47 | 5:27 | 7:08 | 6:01 | 6:15 | 6:35 | 5:23 | 7:14 | 4:47 | 7:43 | 4:43 |
| 22 | 4:55 | 7:47 | 5:28 | 7:07 | 6:02 | 6:13 | 6:36 | 5:22 | 7:16 | 4:46 | 7:43 | 4:44 |
| 23 | 4:56 | 7:46 | 5:29 | 7:05 | 6:03 | 6:11 | 6:38 | 5:20 | 7:17 | 4:46 | 7:44 | 4:44 |
| 24 | 4:57 | 7:45 | 5:30 | 7:03 | 6:04 | 6:09 | 6:39 | 5:19 | 7:18 | 4:45 | 7:44 | 4:45 |
| 25 | 4:58 | 7:44 | 5:31 | 7:02 | 6:05 | 6:07 | 6:40 | 5:17 | 7:19 | 4:44 | 7:45 | 4:46 |
| 26 | 4:59 | 7:43 | 5:32 | 7:00 | 6:06 | 6:06 | 6:41 | 5:16 | 7:20 | 4:44 | 7:45 | 4:46 |
| 27 | 5:00 | 7:42 | 5:34 | 6:59 | 6:07 | 6:04 | 6:43 | 5:14 | 7:22 | 4:43 | 7:45 | 4:47 |
| 28 | 5:01 | 7:41 | 5:35 | 6:57 | 6:08 | 6:02 | 6:44 | 5:13 | 7:23 | 4:43 | 7:45 | 4:48 |
| 29 | 5:02 | 7:40 | 5:36 | 6:55 | 6:10 | 6:00 | 6:45 | 5:12 | 7:24 | 4:42 | 7:46 | 4:48 |
| 30 | 5:03 | 7:39 | 5:37 | 6:54 | 6:11 | 5:59 | 6:46 | 5:10 | 7:25 | 4:42 | 7:46 | 4:49 |
| 31 | 5:04 | 7:37 | 5:38 | 6:52 | | | 6:48 | 5:09 | | | 7:46 | 4:50 |

U.S. Naval Observatory

# Wind Chill Table

## Air Temperature (°F)

| Wind Speed (miles per hour) | 35 | 30 | 25 | 20 | 15 | 10 | 5 | 0 | -5 | -10 | -15 | -20 | -25 | -30 | -35 | -40 | -45 |
|---|---|---|---|---|---|---|---|---|---|---|---|---|---|---|---|---|---|
| | WIND CHILL INDEX — (EQUIVALENT TEMPERATURE) — Equivalent in cooling power on exposed flesh | | | | | | | | | | | | | | | | |
| 4 | 35 | 30 | 25 | 20 | 15 | 10 | 5 | 0 | -5 | -10 | -15 | -20 | -25 | -30 | -35 | -40 | -45 |
| 5 | 32 | 27 | 22 | 16 | 11 | 6 | 0 | -5 | -10 | -15 | -21 | -26 | -31 | -36 | -42 | -47 | -52 |
| 10 | 22 | 16 | 10 | 3 | -3 | -9 | -15 | -22 | -27 | -34 | -40 | -46 | -52 | -58 | -64 | -71 | -77 |
| 15 | 16 | 9 | 2 | -5 | -11 | -18 | -25 | -31 | -38 | -45 | -51 | -58 | -65 | -72 | -78 | -85 | -92 |
| 20 | 12 | 4 | -3 | -10 | -17 | -24 | -31 | -39 | -46 | -53 | -60 | -67 | -74 | -81 | -88 | -95 | -103 |
| 25 | 8 | 1 | -7 | -15 | -22 | -29 | -36 | -44 | -51 | -59 | -66 | -74 | -81 | -88 | -96 | -103 | -110 |
| 30 | 6 | -2 | -10 | -18 | -25 | -33 | -41 | -49 | -56 | -64 | -71 | -79 | -86 | -93 | -101 | -109 | -116 |
| 35 | 4 | -4 | -12 | -20 | -27 | -35 | -43 | -52 | -58 | -67 | -74 | -82 | -89 | -97 | -105 | -113 | -120 |
| 40 | 3 | -5 | -13 | -21 | -29 | -37 | -45 | -53 | -60 | -69 | -76 | -84 | -92 | -100 | -107 | -115 | -123 |
| 45 | 2 | -6 | -14 | -22 | -30 | -38 | -46 | -54 | -62 | -70 | -78 | -85 | -93 | -102 | -109 | -117 | -125 |

COLD

VERY COLD

BITTER COLD

EXTREME COLD

WIND SPEEDS GREATER THAN 40 MPH HAVE LITTLE ADDITIONAL CHILLING EFFECT

EXAMPLE: A 30 mile-per-hour wind, combined with a temperature of 30 degrees Fahrenheit (-1 degree Celsius), can have the same chilling effect upon you as a temperature of -2 degrees Fahrenheit (-19 degrees Celsius), when the wind is calm.

National Oceanic and Atmospheric Administration

"BUFFALO CHIPS"          *STANTON*

# Gone With the Wind

If it wasn't tied down securely, chances are it was carried off by the hurricane force gusts that slammed into the Western New York region on Thursday, February 27,1997.

The "high wind" event had gusts clocked as high as 81 mph at the Niagara Falls airport. It forced the closing of the Skyway, and Youngman Highway. Many trees in the area were uprooted, and several had crashed into homes. Trucks on the Grand Island bridges were being pushed against the guardrails, one truck overturned.

For Daniel and Cynthia Budd of Buffalo, coming home and finding bricks lying on the side of their home was somewhat of a mystery. They had their chimney repaired a few months earlier. The Budds received a phone call from a next door neighbor to tell them that she was terrified that bricks were flying against her house.

That's when the Budds discovered that several layers of bricks, and the chimney cap were knocked off by the limb of their maple tree that stands against their home.

At one time, power authorities throughout the area reported that 100,000 homes were without power. The merciless winds were so powerful that it pushed Lake Erie water levels up by about 6 feet in just a few hours.

The winds collapsed two air supported domes — a golf driving range "bubble" in Wheatfield, where damage was estimated at $1 million, and a new $2 million covered soccer and hockey facility in Lancaster.

# Ice Bridge at Niagara Falls Thickest in Years

The ice bridge at Niagara Falls was at its thickest in as many years during the winter of 1996-'97. The ice bridge, which doesn't look at all like a bridge, is a formation of floes that often jam the river from bank to bank during the dead of winter.

Years ago, it was a popular pastime for people to walk across the ice between the U.S. and Canadian sides of the river. All that came to a halt on February 4, 1912. Three people were swept to their death when an ice bridge formed at the base of the cataracts broke up, and the victims were carried into the rapids in the Niagara River Gorge.

# Deep Space Visitor Spotted in the Sky

The Winter and Spring of 1997, brought many Western New Yorkers' outside to observe the Comet Hale-Bopp. Hale-Bopp, discovered by two backyard astronomers in July, 1995, brightened in the last year and a half on its approach to the inner solar system.

The 25-mile-wide ball of dirt and ice was visible to the naked eye early in the morning, and in the evening sky from late March into early May.

This spectacular celestial scene was enhanced on April 23, when a lunar eclipse darkened the evening sky. Hale-Bopp was even figured in a cult's mass suicide in California. Hale-Bopp was much brighter, and more visible than Halley's Comet which visited us in 1986.

# Weather Wizards Visit the White House

The call went out for 50 weathermen across the nation to trek to Washington to meet President Clinton and Vice President Gore. The topic: global warming.

I was ushered into the White House on September 30, 1997. It goes without saying that security was tight. Fate would have it that I would be the weatherman to set off the White House alarm as I walked through the metal detector!

It turned out that I had an ear pierce in my pocket, the kind used to hear my producer back in Buffalo. The metal clasp on the tiny device sounded the alarm.

Of course, I was red-faced for a moment. But I managed to regain my composure and walked up a flight of stairs to a "green room" where the reception was being held.

We feasted on cookies, wine, iced tea and ice water as we anxiously awaited our opportunity to meet the president. When the moment arrived, I was impressed by his smile and firm handshake. And his impromptu talk on the timely issue of global warming was interesting.

My broadcast from the lawn of the White House was a dream come true. I'm still not certain about the actual warming of the earth, but my experience in Washington is one that I'll never forget.

# Hail, Hail, All the Gang had Fear

Severe thunderstorms raced through Western New York on Friday July 19, 1997. The brief afternoon storms not only brought terrific downpours, but also winds that gusted to 73 mph.

Area residents watched nervously, as the thunderstorm's furious winds knocked down trees, and dropped severe hail which was three-fourths of an inch, or larger, on all eight Western New York counties. The hail that fell in Clarence was the largest recorded, said the National Weather Service.

The combination of lightning strikes, high wind, hail, and heavy downpours in some areas, wreaked havoc in several locations. A direct strike of lightning at the Orchard Park Police Station knocked out computer equipment, but the town's 911 system was still operational.

Firefighters in Buffalo were kept busy when they responded to a fire, caused by a lightning strike at 317 Woodside Avenue. Damage to the home was pegged at $4,000.

# It's Snowing Worms!

It's a meteorological phenomenon which should have made it into *Ripley's Believe it or Not*. The January 13, 1878 edition of the *Buffalo Sunday Recorder* reported that an area of Lockport was deluged with apple worms!

The temperatures fell overnight and the following morning, the ground was covered with wet, sloppy snow.

A local principal noticed that the snow looked odd. Upon closer inspection, he discovered that the "precipitation" consisted mostly of yellowish-white worms with black heads. Thrust under a microscope, these critters were even found to have blood circulating through their veins.

When the snow thawed, the worms lost their shape and seemed to liquefy. Other regions around Western New York reported "wormfalls" at around the same time, but weather gurus have never been able to explain the weird occurrence.

---

## Temperature Tidbit

The summer of '97 ended with no 90 degree day recorded. It was the second summer that did not produce a 90 degree day. The last time Buffalo had a 90 degree day was August 19, 1995. On August 15, 1995, the mercury soared to 97 degrees. Buffalo's all time record of 99 degrees was on August 27, 1948.

# Weather Glossary

**Advisories:** Bad weather that could affect travel and outside activities — i.e., Lake Snow, blowing snow, wind chill — freezing rain.

**Barometer:** A device used to measure air pressure.

**Blizzard Warning:** Either imminent or already starting. Lots of snow — winds faster than 35 mph and visibility of one-quarter mile or less over an extended time period.

**Dewpoint:** Measure of humidity given in terms of temperature at which dew will start to form.

**Doppler Radar:** Radar that measures speed and direction of a moving object.

**Downburst:** Wind blasting down from a thunderstorm or shower.

**Flash Flood:** Flooding with a rapid water rise.

**Front:** Boundary between air masses of different densities, and usually different temperatures.

**Frost:** Water vapor that has turned to ice on an object.

**Graupel:** Form of ice created when supercooled water droplets coat a falling ice crystal.

**Gulf Stream:** A warm ocean current that flows from the Gulf of Mexico across the Atlantic to the European coast. It helps warm Western Europe.

**Jet Stream:** A narrow band of upper atmosphere wind with speeds greater than 57 mph.

**Lightning:** A visible discharge of electricity produced by a thunderstorm.

**National Weather Service:** Federal agency observes and forecasts weather. Formerly the U.S. Weather Bureau. It's part of the National Oceanic and Atmospheric Administration, which is part of the Department of Commerce.

**NEXRAD:** Next Generation Weather Radar system installed in the 1990's by the National Weather Service, the Defense Department and the Federal Aviation Administration.

**Relative Humidity:** The ratio of the amount of water vapor actually in the air compared to the amount the air can hold at its temperature and pressure. This is expressed as a percentage.

**Snow Squall Warning:** This means that squalls will soon begin. Six inches of snow likely in narrow bands. Heavier squalls may produce over 12 inches. Be alert for large bands of snow that occur down wind of Lake Erie, and Lake Ontario. As much as 24" could accumulate. Dependent on wind direction, other parts of WNY may get flurries or sunshine.

**Squall Line:** A squall line is made up of several thunderstorms. It can be more than 100 miles long. Squall lines are often 50 to 150 miles ahead of an advancing cold front.

**Stationary Front:** A warm-cold air boundary with neither cold or warm air advancing.

**Thunder:** Sound produced by a lightning discharge. Sound travels about a mile in 5 seconds. Start counting when you see a lightning flash. If you hear the thunder in 5 seconds, the lightning's a mile away; in 10 seconds it's two miles away.

**Tornado or Severe Thunderstorm Warning:** A severe thunderstorm or a tornado has been spotted locally, take safe shelter immediately!

**Tornado or Severe Thunderstorm Watch:** Conditions are favorable for severe thunderstorms or tornadoes to occur over a broad area.

**Trade Winds:** Global-scale winds in the tropics that blow generally toward the west in both hemispheres.

**Tropical Storm:** A tropical cyclone with 39 to 74 mph winds.

**Unstable Air:** Air in which temperature and moisture are favorable for the creation of updrafts and downdrafts that can create clouds that sometimes grow into thunderstorms. Precipitation will be showery.

**Warm front:** A warm-cold air boundary with the warm air advancing.

**Waterspout:** A tornado or weaker vortex from the bottom of a cloud to the surface of a body of water.

**Wind Chill Factor:** Effect of wind blowing away the warmed air near the body.

**Winter Storm Warning:** Snow, of 6 inches or more is already occurring or likely to occur.

**Winter Storm Watch:** Conditions are favorable for a big snowstorm. These are usually predicted 12 to 48 hours ahead of a storm.

# About the Author

Tom Jolls is a native Western New Yorker, born in Newfane, raised in Lockport, attended North Park Jr. High School and a graduate of Lockport Sr. High School. He attended University of Buffalo, was married in 1955 after serving 2 years in the U.S. Army Signal Corps. He was stationed at Ft. Lewis, Washington, after completing training at the U.S. Signal School in Augusta, GA. He was an announcer for WUSJ in Locport, WBEN Buffalo, and did TV news and weather at Channel 4 from 1963 to 1965 when he was hired at WKBW-TV Channel 7 where he has been employed for 32 years. Married to the former Janice Cronkhite, of Lockport.

The couple has six children and eight grandchildren as of this writing. Tom and Janice enjoy travelling in their motor home, and spending time at their summer place in Friendship, NY in Allegany County. At home in Orchard Park, Tom enjoys taking care of their horses, gardening and playing engineer and conductor with his "LGB" electric train. He has a complete layout with houses, and a tunnel where by the train, leaves the trainroom, disappears for a moment, then re-enters the room at another place. He finds much fun with his weather instruments, where he monitors weather conditions daily.

# About the Collaborator

Joseph A. Van Meer has been a life-long resident of Buffalo living on the West Side. He attended School #56 and graduated in 1972. He enrolled in the Quantity Food Services program at Emerson Vocational High School, where he graduated in 1976.

He became very active in community issues in the mid 1980's and was elected three times as President of Bird-Ashland Residents Block Club. In this capacity he worked with his neighbors, and public officials to help rid his neighborhood of crime, negligent absentee landlords, and drugs.

Recently, Van Meer graduated from Empire State College with a Bachelors Degree in Communications. He is also a member of The Society Of Professional Journalists. Research is Van Meer's forte, especially when it comes to weather, American and Western New York history.

Van Meer became very curious about weather when he and his friend David Lawson would both wonder if it would snow enough to have a day off from school.

# The Birth of a Publishing Firm

*Photo by Matthew Pitts*

Western New York's most innovative publishing company celebrated its 13th anniversary in 1997. Not bad for a firm which sprouted its roots in trivial turf.

The year was 1984 and the trivia craze was taking the nation by storm. Buffalo broadcast journalist Brian Meyer was playing "another" trivia game with some friends when he came up with the notion of creating a game that focused on local people, places and events. *Western New York Trivia Quotient* sold out its first edition in only six weeks.

A year later, Meyer compiled a book of quotations which focused on the feisty reign of Mayor Jimmy Griffin (a follow-up volume was published in 1993 to coincide with Griffin's last year in office.) By 1966, Western New York Wares Inc. was distributing more than 36 local products.

The area's premier publisher of local books and games has distributed more than 90,000 units. About 150 libraries and schools have turned to the company for resource materials on Western New York's rich history.

Western New York Wares Inc. is highly selective about the titles it publishes; it introduces an average of two new titles each year. But the company is always looking for new regional manuscripts. Meyer invites prospective authors to send a one-page summary to his attention.

"We can only publish about five percent of the ideas that are pitched to us in any given year," said Meyer. "But as the largest publisher of Western New York books, we're always eager to hear new ideas."

The firm publishes only non-fiction works with regional themes. It also offers an array of consulting services to local authors who desire to self-publish their own works.

Meyer attended Buffalo Public School #56, St. Joseph's Collegiate Institute and Marquette University. He is managing editor of news at WBEN Radio where he has worked since 1982.

Meyer, a popular speaker on the local lecture circuit, sees a bright future for Western New York Wares Inc. He hopes to expand the firm's list to include at least 50 regional titles by the year 2000.

# OTHER BOOKS DISTRIBUTED BY WESTERN NEW YORK WARES

**The Finger Lakes Revisited** — Shimmering summer waters, vibrant fall colors, crisp winter landscapes and lush spring greenery. All seasons spring to life in this hardcover book which features more than 100 color photographs of all eleven Finger Lakes, including some stunning aerial perspectives. John Francis McCarthy and Linda Bishop McCarthy have captured the region's rich history and tradition.
*ISBN: 0-9623716-3-7*  **$29.95**

**Western New York Weather Guide** — Readers won't want any "winterup-tions" as they breeze through this lively book which focuses on Buffalo's four seasons. Penned by Channel 7 weather guru Tom Jolls with assistance from Brian Meyer and Joseph Van Meer, this first-of-akind guide focuses on humorous, dramatic and historic weather events over the past century.
*ISBN: 1-879201-18-1*  **$7.95**

**A View Through the Lens of Robert L. Smith: Buffalo Bills Photos** — Bills owner Ralph Wilson says the 444 photos in this unique collection "provide enjoyment and touches of nostalgia I wouldn't trade for a first round draft choice." This eye-grabbing photographic journey chronicles the team's ups and downs from its inception in 1960 to the end of the Jim Kelly era.
*ISBN: 1-879201-17-8*  **$26.95**

**Beyond Buffalo: A Photographic Journey and Guide to the Secret Natural Wonders of our Region** —Full-color photographs and informative vignettes showcase 30 remarkable sites in Western New York. Author David Lawrence Reade includes complete directions and tips for enjoying each site.
*ISBN: 10879201-19-4*  **$19.95**

**Exploring Niagara: The Complete Guide to Niagara Falls and Vicinity** — Filled with 77 spectacular full color photos, the guide includes dozens of tours of wineries, canals, waterfalls, mansions and forests. Authors Hans and Allyson Tammemagi also chronicle the history which has shaped our region.
*ISBN: 0-9681815-0-3*  **$14.25**

**Look Who's Adopted!** — This unique book is written for children who are adopted. Penned by local attorney Michael Taheri, the father of two adopted children, this beautifully illustrated book encourages kids to peer into their exciting futures.
*ISBN: 1-879201-21-6*  **$8.95**

**Buffalo Treasures: A Downtown Walking Guide** — Readers are led on a fascinating tour of 25 major buildings. A user-friendly map and dozens of photos and illustrations supplement a text written by Jan Sheridan.
*ISBN: 1-879201-15-1*  **$4.95**

**Church Tales of the Niagara Frontier: Legends, History & Architecture** — This first-of-a-kind book traces the rich history and folklore of the region through accounts of 60 area churches and places of worship. Written by Austin M. Fox and illustrated by Lawrence McIntyre.
*ISBN: 1-879201-13-5*  **$14.95**

**Water Over the Falls: 101 of the Most Memorable Events at Niagara Falls** Daredevils who defied the Mighty Niagara, tragic rock slides and heroic rescues. More than 100 true-to-life tales are vividly recounted by noted local historian Paul Gromosiak.
*ISBN: 1-879201-16-X*  **$5.95**

**Niagara Falls Q & A: Answers to the 100 Most Common Questions About Niagara Falls** — Author Paul Gromosiak spent four summers chatting with 40,000 Falls tourists. This invaluable guide answers the most commonly asked questions.
*ISBN: 0-9620314-8-8*  **$3.95**

**Zany Niagara: The Funny Things People Say About Niagara Falls** — A fun-filled tour of humorous happenings and historical oddities. Penned by Paul Gromosiak and illustrated by John Hardiman.
*ISBN: 1-879201-06-2*  **$4.95**

**Soaring Gulls & Bowing Trees: The History of the Islands Above Niagara Falls** — The magnetism and history of Niagara Falls spring to life in this insightful book by Paul Gromosiak.
*ISBN: 0-9620314-6-1*                                                                  **$9.95**

**Designated Landmarks of the Niagara Frontier** — A riveting look at the region's architectural past. About 100 landmarks spring to life in a book written by Austin Fox and illustrated by Lawrence McIntyre.
*ISBN: 0-9620314-2-9*                                                                  **$13.95**

**Symbol & Show: The Pan-American Exposition of 1901** — An insightful look at perhaps the greatest event in Buffalo history. The 128-page book was written by Austin Fox and illustrated by Lawrence McIntyre.
*ISBN: 0-6816410-4-5*                                                                  **$13.95**

**Rescue of a Landmark: Frank Lloyd Wright's Darwin D. Martin House** — The untold story of the abandonment and rescue of Western New York's most architecturally significant home is recounted by art historian Marjorie L. Quinlan.
*ISBN: 0-9620314-7-X*                                                                  **$9.95**

**Buffalo's Waterfront A Guidebook** — Edited by Tim Tielman, this 72-page guide showcases more than 100 shoreline sites. The work includes a special fold-out map. Published by the Preservation Coalition of Erie County.
*ISBN: 1-879201-00-3*                                                                  **$5.95**

**The World According to Griffin: The End of an Era** — Compiled by veteran broadcast journalist Brian Meyer, this almanac includes hundreds of ''Griffinisms'' from one of the most feisty mayors in Buffalo history.
*ISBN: 1-879201-11-9*                                                                  **$5.95**

**The A-to-Z Bus Tour of Buffalo (and Beyond)** — This coloring book takes youngsters on an exciting alphabetical tour of Western New York. Seven-year-old Chrisein Ratzel co-authored the book with Brian Meyer. Grand Island artist Anna Finkel illustrated it.
*ISBN: 1-879201-10-0*                                                                  **$3.50**

**The Cheap Gourmets' Dining Guide** — Familiar veterans of local suppertime struggles, Polly and Doug Smith dish out a lively 96-page dining guide.
*ISBN: 1-879201-07-0*                                                                  **$5.95**

**Buffalo City Hall: Americanesque Masterpiece** — Local Historian John Conlin has penned this authoritative guide which chronicles the history and architectural significance of this regional icon.
*ISBN: 1-879201-14-3*                                                                  **$5.95**

**Buffalo Chips: The Book** — More than 100 rib-tickling entrees from local cartoonist Tom Stratton.
*ISBN: 0-9620314-3-7*                                                                  **$4.95**

**Kid's First: A First Aid Guide For Kids** — An educational book for youngsters from age 5 to 10 and their families. Authored by registered nurses Beth Kent-Astrella and Angie Leonard and illustrated by Carol Kent Williams, the book provides basic first aid information.   *ISBN: 1-879201-12-7*                                      **$4.50**

**Quotable Cuamo: The Mario Years** — An offbeat almanac of political quotes and anecdotes compiled by Mary Murray and Brian Meyer.
*ISBN: 1-879201-03-8*                                                                  **$5.95**

**Hometown Heroes: Western New Yorkers in Desert Storm** — (Brian Meyer and Tom Connolly)   *ISBN: 1-879201-04-6*                                             **$5.95**

**Buffalo: A Bulls Eye View** — An offbeat almanac of local anecdotes.
*ISBN: 0-6816410-5-3*                                                                  **$6.95**

**Buffalo Bluff** — A game of cunning hometown deception.   *ISBN: 0-9620314-5-3* **$6.95**

**Western New York Trivia Quotient** — **More** than 1,300 trivia questions make for a fastpaced game.   *ISBN: 0-9620314-0-2*                                       **$6.95**

ALSO: write to us for information about our customized Buffalo Baskets!

Please include 8% sales tax and $2 for shipping. Or write for a catalog of all regional books and games:

**Western New York Wares Inc.**
Attention: Brian Meyer
P.O. Box 733, Ellicott Station
Buffalo, New York 14205